The Flavor
of
North Beach

The Flavor
of
North Beach

by
Brian St. Pierre and Mary Etta Moose

Chronicle Books / San Francisco

Library of Congress Cataloging in Publication Data
St. Pierre, Brian.
    The flavor of North Beach.
    1. Restaurants, lunch rooms, etc.—California—North Beach
(San Francisco)   2. Italian Americans—California—North Beach
(San Francisco)   I. Moose, Mary Etta.   II. Title.
TX945.S74   647'.95794'61   81-4609
ISBN 0-87701-157-5 (pbk.)   AACR2

Edited by Harper and Vandenburgh.
Book and cover design by Thomas Ingalls.
Composition from Type by Design.
Illustrations by Steve Reoutt.

Chronicle Books
870 Market Street
San Francisco, CA 94102

*Our deepest appreciation to those
who put their waists on the line,*

THE PASTA PATROL:

Donna Ewald
Ron Fonte
Alan Goldman
Judy Hughes
Matt and Karen Kramer
Bill and Eileen LeBlond
Jacqueline Londhair
Dick Partee
Charlot and Norwood Pratt
Tom Slater
Larry Smith
Blanche Streeter
John Taddeucci
Bob and Harolyn Thompson

and several others, similarly heroic,
who prefer to remain unsung.

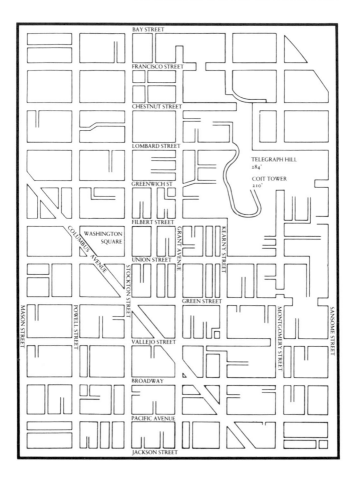

Table of Contents

Introduction 1

A Glossary of North Beach Food Talk 5

Tips on Wine 21

The Restaurants of North Beach 31

　　North Beach Coffeehouses 70

The Food Shops of North Beach 75

　　The Butchers, the Bakers, the Parmesan Graters 77

　　The Delicatessens of North Beach 89

Some North Beach Recipes 97

The Flavor
of
North Beach

Introduction

In the beginning, it really was a beach, just up the shore from Yerba Buena Cove and the rocky slope of Telegraph Hill, and its predominant flavor quickly and thoroughly became Italian.

When gold was discovered late in 1848, the barely established village of San Francisco was set upon by waves of immigrants from all over the world, in one of the largest and certainly craziest booms ever experienced. One of the most difficult trips had to be that of the Italians; for about $120—almost a year's wages at the time— one got the privilege of being crammed into a ship for four, five, or six months, under the ultimate no-frills conditions, and arriving to find he couldn't pick gold nuggets up off the streets after all.

There was, however, an abundance of fish in the Bay, and good earth beneath the sand dunes; gold could be gotten in more familiar ways. The first wave of Italian immigration was made up of Genoese sailors, already familiar with California ports and the new second language; they founded the fishing industry, and were soon followed by their neighbors from Liguria, who planted a variety of vegetables for the first markets and eventually expanded south as far as Half Moon Bay. The Ligurians, hemmed-in between the Apennine Mountains and the sea, had always been noted backyard gardeners—the sight of so much arable soil must surely have convinced them they'd found the Promised Land.

When the ships arrived in the Bay, the eager passengers were frequently joined by the crews, as the ships were abandoned entirely. Several of these ships were turned into hotels, one was the town's first jail, and one, beached at Davis and Pacific streets, became the city's first Italian restaurant, run by Giuseppe Bazzuro.

The streets of San Francisco were a Babel, not only of different languages but of different dialects among supposedly common tongues. Fortunes were made and lost quickly, overnight sometimes, or even on the turn of a card (or a back). Vigilance committees were organized twice, public hangings were popular, and shootouts only faintly resembling duels were common enough on the streets.

There were no garbage dumps; the only sewer system was the streets; rats, fleas, and disease were common. Filling in the Bay at Yerba Buena Cove, east of Montgomery Street, expanded the flatland and made it easier to utilize the abandoned ships, and it also had the virtue of covering up the worst excrescences. There were few homes as such; so, along with gambling halls, brothels, and banks, San

Francisco from the start had a disproportionate number of restaurants for its size.

Through these hectic and difficult years, Italians gained little or no notoriety. They had little power and no major vices, at least not on a scale that made them worth reporting. They worked hard, put down their roots, and sank their money into property, fishing boats, and bringing over more of their own.

The first wave of Italian immigration was composed mostly of northerners, who possessed varied skills and a degree of sophistication. The hard question of assimilation that faced so many immigrants on the East Coast didn't arise for them, as this was such a new and wide-open society, with so many immigrants all at once, that there wasn't anything much to assimilate into—they tended to Italianize the places they settled, rather than the other way round.

Later, there was some immigration from the south of Italy, but the majority of settlers here have been from the north, even into this cen-tury, which explains why we see so little Neapolitan or Sicilian cuisine in San Francisco.

There were pockets of Italian settlement all around San Francisco within a generation, but the largest concentration was in North Beach. When what became Columbus Avenue was cut in 1870, and the Bay continued to be filled in northward, there was even more room to expand and prosper.

The earthquake and fire in 1906 devastated North Beach; Washing-ton Square, formerly its lovely garden, was a tent city for some sur-vivors. But the area was quickly rebuilt, even somewhat sensibly replanned, and a renewed sense of community made it even more Italian in character than ever.

Then, as the city pulled itself together and prepared finally to begin growing up after its long and riotous adolescence, North Beach began to be perceived as a resource—a vital, even raffish, corner of Europe right on the city's doorstep. Here there were theaters where you could see *commedia dell'arte* or opera, lively restaurants, music halls and, later, jazz joints. It was exuberant and maybe a little crazy; it was Bohemia.

And it remains so today, insofar as that spirit can persist; and it does, stubbornly. Carol Doda dances a block away from where Little Egypt danced a couple of generations ago. You can still hear pocket operas at Veneto, keeping alive the tradition of the old Bocce Ball.

And Ferlinghetti tends the literary flame lit by Charles Warren Stoddard, Joaquin Miller, Mark Twain, Bret Harte, and Frank Norris. Two great theaters are now supermarkets and another is a Chinese movie house, but the Club Fugazi is still going, showing "Beach Blanket Babylon," our *commedia dell'arte*, and three new coffeehouses have opened recently, and maybe you ain't seen nothin' yet.

North Beach is fascinating, maddening, sweetly perverse in some places, a pain in the ass in others, its essentially Italianate character somewhat frayed and fragmented now, but still holding up and hanging on. The grin may be rueful, but the abundance and spice and warmth are still there, and it's still a neighborhood, in the best and truest sense of that word.

You ought not to miss it. *B. St. P.*

A Glossary
of North Beach
Food Talk

by Mary Etta Moose

CONTENTS:

Al Dente (ahl dent' ā)

Basilico (bah seal' ēē cō)

Brioschi (brēē ōh' skēē)

Calamari (cah lah mah' rēē)

Calzone (kal zōh' nā)

Cappuccino (kap pŏŏh chēē' nō)

Carciofi (kär chee oh' fēē)

Cioppino (chop pēē' no)

Colomba di Pasquale (kō lum' bah) (dēē) (pahs kuahl' ā)

Crostata (crōw staht' ah)

Dolci / Frutta (dol' chēē) / (fruit' ah)

Fernet Branca (fur net') (brahn' cah)

Finnocchio (fēē nō' kēy ōh)

Formaggio (fore mah' gēē ōh)

Gnocchi (nyōh' kēy)

Mescolonza (mess cō lôn' zah)

Minestrone (min ess trōh' nā)

Panettonne (pan ə tō' nāy)

Pasta (pah' stah)

Pasta Frolla (pah' stah) (frō' lah)

Petrale (pet rah' lay)

Piccata (pēē cah' tah)

Pignoli (pēēn yōh' lēē)

Puntette (po͝on tet′a)

St. Honore (own′ər a)

Sacripantina (sah krē̄e pahn tē̄e′nah)

Semolina (səm ō lē̄e′nah)

Semolo (səm ō′lō)

Spiedini (spāy ē̄e dē̄e′knē̄e)

Spumoni (spo͝oh mō′knē̄e)

Torta di Verdura / Torta di Riso (tor′tah) (dē̄e) (vər do͝or′ah) /

  (tor′tah) (dē̄e) (rē̄′sō)

Vitello (vē̄ tell′ō)

Zabaglione (za bah yō′nā)

Zuccotto (zo͝o cō′tō)

Zuppa Inglese (soup′ah) (ē̄en glā′sāy)

AL DENTE

"To the tooth"; cooked just to the point at which the substance (usually pasta or a vegetable) still offers a slight, pleasant resistance to your bite. Attention to the textures of foods in their preparation is a dividing line between the ordinary and the good Italian cook.

BASILICO (Sweet Basil)

Back before flats sprouted in the front yards of North Beach to accommodate the influx of World War II shipbuilders, the Italian gardens were bigger than the houses and had sheep and chickens and vegetable patches. Today, the cock is still heard to crow and the perfume of basilico prevails in the kitchen gardens of the last Italian holdouts, though I haven't seen a sheep grazing here since 1975, which doesn't mean there aren't a couple of them around somewhere.

The Genovese brought over their own round-leaf variety of basilico seeds—producing leaves the size of limestone lettuce—and have added their accents to the North Beach table. Their pesto sauce for pasta is made with cream instead of oil, and is softer than southern Italy's pungent version.

From July through September, when our sun stays high and hot long enough each day to strengthen the plant's oils, we make batches of "North Beach Pesto Base" for use throughout the year. The basil is picked in the early mornings, while the oils are high in the plant, and is blended with a very little Italian flat-leafed parsley and garlic, and the minimum amount of olive oil needed to bind and preserve it. Stored in small, use-sized containers, it retains its flavor for a good nine months in the deep-freeze. (Faint-hearted out-of-season basil won't do.) Because so little oil is used, and because cheese, nuts, butter, and cream are not added, the flavoring oils are less diminished in storage, and this pesto base is adaptable for use in a great many dishes. See BASIL in the **Recipe Section**, starting on page 104, for the exact proportions of this useful preparation, and recipes for some of the ways to use it.

When used for pasta, a little cream, butter, and pine nuts are blended into this pesto base and it's folded into heated light cream, occasionally with a touch of chicken glacé for more complex flavor. Drained pasta is tossed with butter, then tossed over heat in the creamy pesto and tossed, off-heat, with freshly grated cheese, till every strand of pasta is cheese-coated. Pine nuts, or their popular substitute, walnuts, are optional. Cheese supplies the salt. Hot strands of spaghetti squash can be used instead of pasta. At the local firehouse, they sometimes add fresh spearmint and cream cheese to the pesto, for variety. At Gino & Carlo's saloon, where Genoan Donato Rossi makes the best pesto in town for his bartenders' lunch, sliced potatoes and Italian green beans are sometimes combined with the pasta.

Chef Marcello Persi adds the pesto base with the eggs before mixing in the flour when he makes fresh noodles, for a pale green treat. He combines sweet-red-pepper-flavored pasta with his basil-flavored pasta in a Sauce alla Panna (butter, cheese, and cream) for the Italian Flag Alfredo, or a pretty Christmas-dinner pasta course. He adds a whiff of pesto base to a mixture of Fontina D'Aosta, Bel Paese, Taleggio, and whole-milk ricotta cheeses, to stuff oversize ravioli (cut round with a wine glass), or *agnolotti* (a spoonful of stuffing in the center of pasta rounds, edges moistened and folded into half-moons), or giant pasta shells or manicotti, and puts our local field mushrooms in the panna sauce. Sometimes he uses his basil-flavored pasta dough to make the thin skins for these cheese-stuffed pastas.

We mix a little pesto base and mashed anchovies into a lemony mayonnaise for a chunky salad of tuna, potato, and green beans. The bland local rock cod and sea bass benefit from the flavor boost of a little pesto base in a fresh tomato sauce, a Sauce Aurore, or a Clam Velouté.

The freshly mixed pesto base is also mixed with softened butter and lemon juice to make basil butter, which we roll into logs, wrap, and freeze to slice as needed to serve on broiled fish, grilled chicken or turkey breast, baked potatoes and vegetables. Basil butter spread on crusty Italian corn-flour bread makes a good sandwich with tomato, sweet onion, and Fontina d'Aosta cheese. The pesto base can be added with grated cheese to bread dough for Pesto Rolls, brushed with egg white and sprinkled with pine nuts and butter before baking. A lovely vinaigrette is achieved by adding olive oil to the pesto base, and mixing with pear vinegar, or rice-wine vinegar.

If you are not going to make your own, the best commercial ready-to-use creamy pesto sauce is Ricci brand, available in the frozen-food counters of all the area's delicatessens.

BRIOSCHI

Italian Alka Seltzer.

CALAMARI

Baby squid is one of the most popular North Beach fish. It comes in fresh from Monterey Bay starting in September for several months in a good year, and frozen, from Japan and Mexico thereafter. Calamari survives freezing intact, but requires more attentive timing than the fresh, to retain tenderness.

The mysteries of handling this once-exotic fish have been dispelled by extensive explanatory copy from our conscientious Bay Area food editors. Hence calamari, no longer the dime-a-pound protein for the poor and poets, is a fashionable food for the home cook. It is stuffed with shellfish and braised, or sauteed with mushrooms in a brown Marsala sauce or a tomato sauce, or floured and deep fried, or combined with other seafood in a garlicky tomato sauce for pasta. If you haven't tackled it yet, the simple cleaning procedure awaits your attention in our **Recipe Section** (North Beach Fishermen's Salad).

A new calamari product on the market is slices from the mantles of the bigger squid, tender as abalone if handled and prepared like abalone, dore, in lemon sauce.

CALZONE

Elongated-oval-shaped individual pies, made of pizza dough, stuffed with cheese and meat, and baked (sometimes fried).

CAPPUCCINO

One of the many Italian coffeehouse specialties, this brownish drink was named after the Capuchin friars, because their robes are the same color.

Italian dark roast beans are pulverized and steam-brewed in an espresso machine. The syrupy coffee is combined with an equal amount of milk that has been puffed up with steam. Cappucino is served with sugar and powdered chocolate or cinnamon.

CARCIOFI

Artichokes. They're so plentiful in California that the North Beach gardeners now allow theirs to mature into the showy purple flower-brackets which the fruit becomes. The Italians prize the smallest artichokes during their brief season, July through August. The baby artichoke appears in the local markets from ¾ to 2 inches in diameter. After the prickly tip has been whacked off, the rest is so tender it can be cooked and eaten whole, embryonic choke and all.

This is something for visitors to northern California to keep an eye open for, in both restaurant and delicatessen preparations, as these little artichokes are not shipped far from their growing area. Don't say no if you encounter baby artichoke frittatas, or a sauté of veal, lamb, or chicken with tiny whole artichokes, or even the deep-fried whole ones. They also appear in a vegetable stew, steamed with fat spring onions and fresh fava beans, in olive oil. Mature chokes come in fresh from September through June.

See the **Recipe Section** for Artichoke Frittata and Chicken Jerusalem with Baby Artichokes. Visiting cooks will find it worthwhile to take some home to try.

CIOPPINO

There used to be so much crab around that Rose Evangelisti would make Crabmeatballs (a lotta hard work) and Spaghetti for her special suppers at old Pistolla's, oh, boy!

Time was you could expect your local to be serving *cioppino* (crab stew) to accommodate its Friday night drinkers, whether the saloon served food or not. Our Dungeness crab was plentiful, and the young fishermen and their hot girls presented a Tom Jones scene, standing around the dance floor sucking crab out of their shells over steaming bowls.

Here's a dish not to pass up when you encounter it in the shell, and with the hope that you'll be inspired to try it yourself at home, the authentic North Beach recipe is waiting for you on page 122.

COLOMBA DI PASQUALE

Easter Doves: a slightly sweetened, citron-studded egg bread, shaped like a dove, topped with almond paste and pine nuts.

CROSTATA

Italian Pie Crust, for both main course and dessert pies. Italian crusts differ from American ones in their use of butter and eggs instead of fat and water. If the crust is for a dessert, it also includes a little sugar, fresh lemon zest, and flavoring of Marsala wine or vanilla. The word for the dough used in the crust is *pasta frolla*.

DOLCI/FRUTTA

The dessert course. The most wonderful *dolce* of my memory was a tree-ripened August peach, sliced into a glass of Red Libarle's late-harvest Zinfandel, taken as soon as combined, while the tastes were just getting acquainted. We're so blessed here, with the delights of our pastry shops, and sweets from the delicatessens, and fresh fruits from close-by orchards all year long, and the fine cheeses (when you've got Mascarpone cheese to spoon a little Green Chartreuse over, who needs dessert?), that our homemade desserts are mostly custards, creams, and fruits. Recipes for Fried Cream and a Baked Stuffed Pear are given in the **Recipe Section**. Ideas for assembling desserts are scattered throughout the food section.

FERNET BRANCA

While Brioschi will bubble away acid stomach, Fernet soothes not only digestive dismay, but also a confused liver. When an Italian's indiscretion insults his innards, he knows his penance is to quaff this vile-tasting stuff down straight, with a water or ginger-ale chaser as his absolution. If you don't suffer the Italian guilt, ask for a creme de menthe float on yours. Any North Beach bartender will fix you up.

FINNOCCHIO

In the peasant parlance, the word is an idiom meaning "neither vegetable nor fruit." Forgetting for one moment the effete showmen of the North Beach nightclub of the same name, finnocchio (fennel, or sweet anise) seems to lie dormant in the North Beach soil, awaiting its curtain call. It crops up wild wherever the concrete's removed to house a street tree, and its ferny tops wave "ciao" from any place that hasn't been filled with concrete yet.

In its restaurant appearances, it's mostly gone to seed, and gives its licorice flavor to the "sweet" sausages, which in turn flavor the meat sauces and stuffings, or which are braised with red cabbage or baked in red wine and served with polenta.

In wintertime the celery-like bulb appears in the markets, to braise, or bake *parmigiano*, or add to beef stew or creamed fish soup, or to chill and slice in its lovely cross-section of delicate patterns and several soft shades of green, and serve with a squeeze of fresh lime (good with prosciutto) as a crudité, to please eye and palate. The **Recipe Section** offers it combined with chicken in a salad, and in a pork and fennel duo.

FORMAGGIO

Cheese. Though the city's wine and cheese shops may be stealing some thunder from the cheese counters of North Beach, this is still a smart place to shop for Italian cheeses, not only for the clerks' knowledge of how to include them in your menu, or the wealth of other Italian provender accompanying them in the shops, but mainly because you can count on some of these costly, rare cheeses to be in top shape in these stores. The demand for them is here, and they are not competing with a vast array of other cheeses which might delay their sale. When word gets out that the *torta's* in at Gloria's, it doesn't sit around. That's Torta San Gaudenzia: Mascarpone layered with Italy's gentle blue cheese, Gorgonzola—a splendid taste combination. Mascarpone is Italy's great cream cheese, closer to cream than to cheese. It's delicious plain, or with a dab of preserved fruit. Mixed with raw egg yolk, prosciutto bits, and parmesan cheese, it's a fine coating for fettuccine.

Look for Fontina D'Aosta, the pale orange-brown waxed wheel so superior to all its cousins; Reggiano Parmigiano, the best Parmesan; Cacciocavallo, four-year-old grating cheese, and many others, all selected and held with Italian respect.

Taste before you buy a large cut of any cheese, as tastes vary with the season and what the animal was eating at the time.

GNOCCHI

Small dumplings made of egg and semolina, rice, cornmeal, cream cheese, or potatoes. Gnocchi are boiled and served like pasta, with saucy braised meats, or butter and cheese, or creamy pesto sauce, or meat or tomato sauce. They can be wonderful or terrible, as they must be made with a very light hand.

THE JOE'S SPECIAL

We can't blame the cooks for this North Beach creation. It was invented by a hungry bandleader, Fortune Nelson "Bunny" Burson, late one night in 1932 at New Joe's on Broadway. Bunny had just finished a show at Finnocchio's next door, and when the cook told him there was nothing left but a little hamburger, some spinach, and a couple of eggs, he said "Mix 'em together." Hardly an epicurean delight. The best explanation for the popularity of the Joe is that it's one of those comforting foods. It slides down easily, assuages the innards, and provides nourishment without interrupting the conversation. See the **Recipe Section** for the vegetarian version of the Joe.

MESCOLONZA

This word may be so esoteric that it's known only to the Piemontese. It's a peasant term meaning "a mixture of this and that," and refers to the mixture of liqueurs used, as far as my research revealed, solely to achieve the characteristic dusky taste of the two traditional Piedmont Christmas tortas, made year-round in North Beach, the Torta di Verdura and the Torta di Riso (which see, in the **Glossary** and in **Food Shops**). Mescolonza is bottled commercially and is available at Rossi's Market, but I can't imagine who's buying it, as all the torta makers I've spoken to say they have their own secret formula, and that the bottled product contains too much anise. Italo Lucchesi says the best torta makers have friends who own saloons, as the "right" mixture takes experimentation that's too expensive for the layman. Now you know.

MINESTRONE

Vegetable soup with beans, from a light soup of vegetables cooked in chicken broth with proscuitto bone and cranberry beans, to the down-home deep concoctions a spoon stands up in. The **Recipe Section** contains a classic minestrone you can make at home, when you can't make it to the Beach.

PANETTONE

A slightly sweetened dome-shaped bread, with raisins and candied fruits, usually baked on Wednesdays. It is taken as is when first cut, toasted later. Pannetonne makes good bread pudding, french bread, tea sandwiches, and poultry stuffings. It can be sliced and dried out in a 200° oven, to become a rusk for tea or wine. The dried rusks are good soaked in brandy, milk, sugar, and egg, then grilled in butter. Pannetonne holds well in the freezer if sliced and frozen while still fresh.

PASTA

Unleavened dough, made of various flours and water, sometimes with egg, olive oil, and/or a flavoring puree. It is rolled out, the thinner the better, and cut into a remarkable diversity of forms. Pasta is mostly boiled in water and sauced, or stuffed; or added to soups and casseroles; or steamed in flavored liquid, like rice; or stuffed with savory or sweet farces and deep fried.

There must be a nationwide explosion of interest in pasta, or why are they suddenly making all those expensive, ambitious pasta machines? Is America tired of Franco American? Will we be able to walk our streets at night, secure in the knowledge that behind those lighted windows, somebody is cranking out homemade pasta? One hopes. North Beach is down to only five shops that retail fresh pasta daily (Florence, Cafferata, Italian Village Delicatessen, Molinari, and Panelli). Take some home, sauce it with anything from hamburger to Swan's fresh caviar, it can't be anything but good. If you're a little old pasta maker, see page 106 for Chef Marcello Persi's new idea—pasta made with the sweet basil in it, as well as on it; or let one of North Beach's dozens of Italian restaurants show you what they can do with one of the world's most versatile foodstuffs.

PASTA FROLLA

Dough used for Italian pie crusts. See "Crostata" for full explanation.

PETRALE

A large flounder (*Eopsetta jordani*) found only off the Pacific Coast but all the way from northern Mexico up to Alaska. It is available here fresh any day the boats can go out. It is also marketed in frozen fillets, but petrale loses some of its flavor and texture in the thawing process.

Petrale is Numero Uno among the Pacific flatfishes. (The thinner flounders, sand dabs and rex sole, are #2 and #3, respectively). Our fishermen say it's so sweet and delicate tasting and juicy textured because it swims so deep in the water. Neptune's reasons be what they may, petrale is one of the world's great fishes. We urge visitors from the East Coast and the Gulf Coast, justifiably proud and fond as you are of the products of your native waters, to treat yourselves to some carefully prepared fresh petrale here, before you firm up your position on West Coast fish.

The classic North Beach preparation is to dore the fillets (dip in egg beaten with flour), pan grill until medium rare, and lightly coat with a lemon butter sauce heightened with brandy and capers.

PICCATA

Thin slices of meat or fish, seasoned and floured, or dipped in egg beaten with flour (dore), sautéed in butter, and finished with lemon juice, butter and parsley.

Veal scaloppini are the traditional meat for a piccata, but other foods lend themselves delectably to this preparation: flattened slices of chicken or turkey breast (also good combined with veal); sliced and sweated eggplant; fillets of sole; calamari steaks; deep sea scallops, pounded flat.

The piccata flavor can be made more piquant by adding, during the finishing, a splash of vermouth and brandy and, after reducing the liquid, a sprinkle of capers. Or the flavor can be heightened, according to ingredients, with a bit of chicken glacé or a compound fish butter. Save some poaching butter from your next shad roe, and use it to finish a sea scallops piccata.

PIGNOLI

Pine nuts: the kernels which come from the Italian Stone Pine. As of this writing, they are retailing for six dollars per pound. Their delicate taste and subtle texture set them apart from the less costly nuts, like walnuts, which are being used now as substitutes. Pine nuts are a frequent ingredient in Italian cuisine.

PUNTETTE

An elongated rice-grain-shaped pasta, cooked like rice. Variations of this tiny pasta are Orzo, Risone, Risino, Rosamarina, Semi di Melone (melon seeds), Semi di Mele (apple seeds).

SACRIPANTINA

A North Beach dessert made exclusively by Stella Pastry. (See the **Food Shops** section for greater detail.) The word is said to translate, loosely, as "Oh, how marvelous!" It's on the dessert lists of a restaurant and a coffeehouse here, and available at retail from Stella. It tastes best when made in the dome shape, because this gives the best proportions of cake to custard. Restaurants will order it for your party.

ST. HONORE

A cake for celebrations: a pastry shell filled with custard cream and sometimes frangipane, and ringed with little cream puffs and icing roses. It is available from Stella Pastry and from Victoria. The restaurants will order it for your party, upon request.

SEMOLINA

The pasta flour milled from durum wheat, the hard winter wheat, always available in all North Beach delicatessens.

SEMOLO

Whole-wheat bread flour.

SPIEDINI

Any combination of foods, threaded on skewers, marinated and basted with their cooking substances, grilled or roasted. A couple of examples of choice North Beach speidini are: with morsels of rib eye of veal and pancetta rotolata; and another combining green onions and cherry tomatoes with chunks of our local Pacific salmon in season which are marinated in olive oil with a little lemon juice and vermouth and crushed fennel seeds, salt and pepper, and grilled, basting with marinade, until the fish is medium rare.

SPUMONI

More than one flavor of ice cream, in any combination, layered, and studded with candied fruit, and sometimes crushed caramelized nuts.

TORTA DI RISO AND TORTA DI VERDURA

The traditional Tuscan Christmas tortas: a *pasta frolla* crust with egg and a Mescolonza liqueur, filled with a dense, dusky pudding. The Verdura, from the town of Lucca, contains swiss chard, raisins, pine nuts, eggs, bread, and the Mescolonza. The Riso, from the town of Florence, is a chocolate nut rice pudding with Mescolonza. Both are made year-round at Cuneo and Danilo bakeries.

VITELLO

Veal. After it's cooked, the macho Italians change its gender from masculine to feminine and call it *vitella*.

For years, North Beach butcher Bruno Iacopi has wondered aloud, and I do mean aloud, how long it would take our leading food writers to catch on to the fact that "rose" veal has more flavor than "the white." Only now are our mange-mavens beginning to chew on the notion.

The most costly veal is produced, in quantities inadequate for the growing demand, from calves called "vealers," kept penned in stalls to curb the spread of disease in these anemic animals, and fed only milk and iron-free milk replacers made from milk products, until the meat is mature enough to pass government inspection for slaughter as "milk-fed" veal—depending upon breed, anywhere from two weeks (a big holstein calf) to eight weeks (small dairy breeds). This is the European-style milk-fed veal, known around here as "the white." It is generally prized for its creamy pink color and the tenderness of its unused muscles. In our neck of the woods, it is thought to have less taste than what we call "the rose."

There is considerable confusion about the difference between "milk-fed vealers" and "calves." The U.S. Department of Agriculture defines a vealer as being not over three months of age, subsisting largely on milk and milk replacer, and having light, greyish-pink meat. This is our "Second Stage Rose," the animals still kept penned and on milk replacer, but not slaughtered until they are from nine to twelve weeks old (depending upon breed). It is still milk-fed veal, but the color has developed from creamy pink to greyish, deeper pink, and the flavor has developed along with the color.

Veal is the most difficult meat to cook, because of its high moisture content. If not timed precisely, it goes from tender to chewy in an instant, and once it goes, it dries out in the cooking before it becomes chewable again. There is less moisture in the "rose" veal, and it performs with less temperament than younger veal.

After the third month, the animal is now officially a calf, and the meat is Baby Beef, not veal. When you shop for veal, remember that the only bright red flesh in a vealer is his vital organs.

Restaurants in North Beach offer many veal preparations—dozens of scaloppine, saltimbocca, spiedini, osso buco, rolled stuffed roasts, cutlets, chops, many braises and sautés, sweetbreads, brains, kidneys, and calves livers. The **Recipe Section** offers three ideas.

In North Beach, Little City Market carries rose veal; Washington Square Market carries the white.

ZABAGLIONE

A labor of love. No machine makes a proper zabaglione, save the tough arm of a cook who's all the while hoping no one sees yours and wants him to do it again. It's egg yolks and sugar and dry Marsala wine, or sherry, with air whisked into it over flame until it's transmuted into a pale yellow foam of tingling warmth. If you can't leave well enough alone, pour it over a few fresh raspberries or slices of ripe peach, or both. With whipped cream folded in, and usually an orange liqueur flavoring instead of Marsala, it's used as a filling for cakes made of liqueur-sprinkled *genoise* (sponge) or lady fingers, or it is frozen in molds, with any of a variety of liqueur flavorings.

ZUCCOTTO

Another of those dome-shaped sweets. The Italian pastry chef is partial to the dome, inspired by Italy's basilicas (church domes). This one is spongecake layered with buttercream, filberts, and candied fruit, with maraschino liqueur spooned over the top; Victoria Pastry has a freezerful of them at all times.

ZUPPA INGLESE

English soup—Italy's elaborate interpretation of the English trifle, served on festive occasions. Victoria Pastry's no-holds-barred zuppa has spongecake soaked with cherry liqueur and rum, vanilla zabaglione custard, whipped cream, candied cherries, and icing roses. Stella Pastry's gossamer version is thin slices of vanilla and chocolate *genoise* layered with a solid, Mascarpone-like cream, coated with faintly sweetened whipped cream, and adorned with macaroons and pale chocolate festoons.

Tips on Wine

by Brian St. Pierre

It was a Frenchman who declared that "a meal without wine is like a day without sunshine." To any Italian, that was merely a case of stating the obvious.

California wine was part of the flavor of North Beach from the start. Many of the would-be Forty-Niners from Italy (and other countries) soon learned that they could make a living more comfortably in a winery or kitchen than up in the rough hills, and they were soon doing what they knew best.

In those days, wine from the area surrounding San Francisco was laboriously hauled in in large casks and delivered straight to the restaurants, often by the winemaker himself. Many of these pioneers remained anonymous; it was their sons who put their names on labels years later—names which still resound today.

Any house in North Beach that had a basement was likely to have a cask of its own homemade wine; it was said that the heady aroma of fermenting wine in October and November every year was pervasive. After the earthquake in 1906, most of the wine went to putting out the Great Fire, sparing the area from destruction.

Affectionately known as "Dago Red," this wine was frequently a blend of several grapes, and was inexpensive and ubiquitous. During Prohibition, religious institutions were exempt from the general ban on wine and, according to some historians, quite a few North Beach homes became "churches."

With Repeal and the opening of the Golden Gate Bridge, a good selection of wine was available in North Beach. Bottled wine proudly bearing the names of its makers was the order of the day. Today, many of the same names predominate. Wine lists in North Beach are generally good, but conservatively drawn, within a narrow range of familiar (and Italian) names.

What about matching up food and wine? Some people seem to think that there is only one "correct" wine for each dish, which is arrant nonsense. Others stick with the tried-and-true "red with meat, white with fish and chicken" approach, which is perhaps better but still not on the mark. Obviously it would be folly to drink a light white wine with a tomato/garlic-sauced red-meat dish that would utterly cancel out the wine, but there are plenty of other choices—a lot of Italian food (especially northern Italian) lends itself to a variety of wines.

The basic thing to bear in mind is flavor types, and especially flavor intensities. If baked chicken in a simple sauce rates a five on a scale of one to ten, then it calls for a light, probably white, wine that is also a five. This might be a California Johannisberg Riesling or Chenin

Blanc, or an Italian Soave or Frascati. Baking the chicken in a richer sauce, perhaps a butter and herb sauce, would raise the intensity and call for a Fumé Blanc or Chardonnay from California or a Pinot Grigio from Italy. A tomato-and-garlic sauce could tip the bird over into the red-wine column.

Veal dishes lend themselves to a wide range of preparations, and thus to a wide range of wines—you can hardly go wrong with any dry wine you like. Shellfish, with their more pronounced flavors, call for sturdy white wines, even if there's a tomato sauce involved, because their tartness and chilliness clean and refresh your palate.

Basically, however, it should never be too much of a problem. Italian foods were made for wine.

CALIFORNIA WINE TYPES: REDS

Cabernet Sauvignon

This wine sits comfortably and easily at the top of the wine ladder—the grape makes some of the best wines in the world. The flavors, as befits a classic, are complex; it is noted for a mouth-puckering, astringent quality. Some find it herbaceous, similar perhaps to fresh basil. There is also a pleasantly vegetative undertone to the taste that is reminiscent of fresh green peppers.

These are somewhat clumsy attempts to define a fleeting set of impressions that, in the best Cabernets, come together in the aroma and on the palate. Let's just say that, when matched up with full-flavored beef or lamb dishes, Cabernet Sauvignon is the ultimate packager of a meal.

Pinot Noir

Ideally, Pinot Noir is soft, even velvety in texture, with a pleasant fullness and a slight tang in the flavor. Pinot Noirs tend not to be too acidic, and so make a good match with a variety of foods.

Gamay and Gamay Beaujolais

The two grapes are not relatives, though in their former home, in France, they were at least neighbors. The Gamay Beaujolais turns out to be a misidentified strain of Pinot Noir; Gamay, sometimes also called Napa Gamay, is the "true" grape of Beaujolais.

The matter is not as complicated as it could be, simply because both grapes are made into light and lively wines meant for easy and early drinking, with more similarities than differences between them—casual wines for casual meals.

Petite Sirah

This grape comes from the Rhone Valley of France, but makes a very uniquely Californian wine, ample and fleshy—a Rubens of a wine. Petite Sirahs tend to be deep in color, and astringent, and they possess a slight spiciness in their refreshing aftertaste. They go well with the fullest-flavored meats.

Barbera

This grape came originally from the Piedmont region of Italy, and makes a similar wine here—tart, slightly astringent, and rather assertive. This is a rough-and-ready wine, great with pizza, spaghetti and meatballs, or lasagna.

Zinfandel

The origins of Zinfandel—often billed as "California's mystery grape"—are obscure, but there is no mystery as to its popularity: it can make awfully good wine, in a variety of styles. It's safe to say that there is a Zinfandel for everyone's taste. (And the current theory as to its origin centers on Italy, which may explain why it works so well with so many Italian dishes.)

Zinfandel has been styled as "America's Beaujolais," a characterization which is more handy than accurate—Zinfandel is rather more tart than Beaujolais. The similarities lie in the lightness of the wines and their refreshing quality. The late August Sebastiani used to say, "It's a wine you can keep coming back to without ever getting tired of it."

California winemakers, always experimenting, try variations on the basic style, sometimes making it heavier or more tannic, but the basic grace note that is always struck is a kind of wild-blackberry flavor that is enormously appealing.

CALIFORNIA WINE
TYPES: WHITES

Chardonnay

If Cabernet Sauvignon is the king of wines, Chardonnay is easily the queen. People trying to define the full-bodied quality of the wine frequently resort to the word "buttery," merely as a metaphor for its richness. I prefer to be reminded of the tartness and intensity of a good cold-weather apple, like a Mackintosh at the peak of ripeness, at least as a starting point—there's a lot more to the flavor.

A wine this special might be wasted on an average dish. The best fish and shellfish preparations are always enormously enhanced by a Chardonnay.

Sauvignon Blanc / Fumé Blanc

Two different names, but the wine is from the same grape, and it is only a little less intense and complex than Chardonnay, and so should be matched with the same kinds of foods. Its flavor is described as "grassy," and it does evoke those childhood summer days when you chewed on a long blade of grass from the lawn you were supposed to have mown hours earlier. It goes well with some veal dishes, especially the ones featuring lemon and butter.

Chenin Blanc

Basically a light and fruity wine, meant to be enjoyed for its youthful charms, with a slightly flowery aroma, and a straightforward, uncomplicated flavor. A good companion for chicken or for simply-prepared fish.

French Colombard

Also a light wine meant to be drunk young, with a trifle less character than Chenin Blanc, but distinguished by a shade more tartness and, usually, dryness.

Johannisberg Riesling

In California, this grape has usually been made into wines which are drier than their German counterparts, but that has been changing for a little while now. Johannisberg Riesling usually lacks the acidity to go well with fish, but it is generally a terrific match with chicken. It is characterized by a fresh and flowery aroma that reminds some of apricots or peaches and, usually, slight sweetness or fruitiness.

CALIFORNIA WINE TYPES: ROSÉS

Rosé

This wine has suffered for a long time by being thought of as a compromise wine for people who didn't know what to order—a little pink wine for the little lady, perhaps? It has also been unnecessarily reviled by wine snobs. Luckily, winemakers and the general public have paid no attention, and today we have more good wine of this type than ever.

The rosés which go well with Italian foods are generally those made from specific grape types: that is, Rosé of Pinot Noir, Zinfandel Rosé, Gamay Rosé, etc. These tend to be dry and flavorful and go well with light and simple dishes.

ITALIAN WINES

Italian wines have become quite popular in the United States recently, surpassing by far the French and German imports. One reason is that they are frequently not expensive; also, many of the technical innovations that distinguish California wines have shown up in Italy—notably cold fermentation (which brings out the flavors of the grapes) and the use of stainless-steel tanks, which preserves the wines' freshness.

The Italian attention to winemaking detail has not, however, been matched by any zeal for tidying up label nomenclature. An Italian wine may be known by the principal grape, as in California, but it may also be named after the town or district in which it was produced, or something merely fanciful in Latin; additionally, the same grape may have a different name in another province which also believes in varietal labeling.

Further, some words, such as *classico*, may mean nothing at all, or a great deal. Luckily for us, not all of the multitude of Italian wines are imported into America, and a number of generalizations about the principal types apply well enough for an orientation.

First, some label language: *rosso* (red), *bianco* (white), *rosato* (rosé), *secco* (dry), *abboccato* or *amabile* (semi-sweet), *dolce* (sweet), *frizzante* (slightly sparkling), *spumante* (sparkling), *cantina sociale* (cooperative cellar), *imbottigliato* (bottled), and *vendemmia* (vintage).

All imported wines marketed in the United States bear a red seal with the letters I.N.E., which merely indicates that the wines have met the standards of the import laws applicable to this country, and insures their authenticity. It is *not* a guarantee of quality.

Similarly, the words *Denominazione di Origine Controllata* appear on many labels; they mean that the wine has met certain stipulated standards relating to the style of the area, cultivation practices in the vineyards, blending, bottling specifications, alcohol levels, and aging requirements. D.O.C. wines account for about one-third of all Italian wines imported into the United States, and though they can generally be assumed to be better than non-D.O.C. wines, the appellation is not a guarantee of quality.

The most popular Italian wine in America is Lambrusco, which is a slightly sweet, slightly fizzy, and thoroughly silly wine, known often as "Bologna cola." It's Italy's answer to Cold Duck, and not worth discussion.

ITALIAN WINE TYPES: REDS

Barbaresco

One of the better types generally, from the Piedmont area in northwestern Italy; astringent and tart, medium-bodied, best with a little age, say at least five years after the vintage.

Barbera

Somewhat different from the California version usually—somewhat more acidic and full-bodied (almost too much so sometimes). Usually good but never great.

Bardolino

One of the most popular Italian wines, this is a light red wine in both color and body, from the north of Italy. It tends to be tart, even sharp, and is best consumed when fairly young. An uncomplicated wine.

Barolo

This wine vies with the best Chianti Classicos for the title of the best
red wine of Italy, and it generally comes out a little ahead. It tends to
be full-bodied, deep in color, aged several years in wood before bottling, and best with several years' aging in the bottle.

Chianti and Chianti Classico

Chianti acquired a bad name over the years because of so much poorly
made, almost sour wine that came in those familiar straw-wrapped
bottles—it was correctly perceived as the other "Dago Red." Often
the wine was cheaper than the bottle and straw wrapping. Those days
are over, and Chianti today is generally a medium-bodied, piquant,
straightforward wine. A little bit of white wine is blended into it,
contributing a pleasant lightness.

Chianti Classico is quite a step up, like an older brother who got all
the looks, talent, and charm; there is a family resemblance, but that's
all. Classicos are well-balanced, full-bodied, often complex wines that
age well as a rule. There has been some vineyard expansion in the
inner zone of the region, and some Classicos have been a little lighter
recently than in the past, perhaps catering to the export trade, which
wants wines that do not have to be laid down for additional aging.

Ghemme

There is not a lot of this full-bodied wine around, but it's worth
trying if you find it. A powerful wine that shouldn't even be opened
until it is at least ten years old, Ghemme is complex, astringent,
mouth-coating. It could only go with the richest foods; it is superb
after dinner, with cheeses.

Valpolicella

The most popular respectable Italian red in America, it is light in color
and body, but is usually an agreeable bottle of wine. Ideally it is tangy
and fresh, with a clean aftertaste. There are, bascially, two styles: the
majority fit the above description; Valpolicella Superiore has additional
wood aging before bottling.

ITALIAN WINE TYPES: WHITES

Frascati

A fairly delicate wine, from near Rome, this tends to be more of a wine to drink as an aperitif or on a warm afternoon; most foods would overpower its lightness.

Orvieto

Also a light wine; in Italy, it is made in dry and semi-sweet versions, but for export it is generally dry. It tends to have a nice tartness about it, and the better versions can be quite fruity.

Pinot Grigio

A medium-bodied wine, also somewhat tart, somehow possessing character without a lot of complexity—a straightforward wine that goes well with many foods. The better ones are among Italy's best white wines today.

Soave

Probably the best-known Italian white, it also used to be among the best. Today, with a booming market in white wine in America, a lot of second-rate versions seem to be flooding the market. A light, dry wine, it is rarely disagreeable; the good ones are clean and fresh, and all should be consumed when young.

Verdicchio

This wine comes in the tall green amphora-shaped bottle, and frequently is a good match with fish, if the fish is simply prepared, as the wine is light, tending to be pale, dry, and fresh-tasting.

The Restaurants of North Beach

by Brian St. Pierre

I should begin by explaining the premise here. I have left out pizza parlors and a few other places which don't quite possess the Italianate/Bohemian character of North Beach. I've sought, in this section, to find the menu selections that best express the variety of the cuisines of Italy, always seeking the unique, aiming to provide you with guideposts to what we hope will be a culinary adventure. The specific dishes I highlight are either house specialties or among the best of many versions of more standard recipes.

The flavor of North Beach extends beyond its borders, of course; it is holding its own in pockets of the Mission district and on Chestnut Street in the Marina, and another generation is thriving in Marin County. There is an Original Joe's downtown and one on Chestnut Street, both preserving the Joe's style, and there are others around town. (As Herb Caen once observed, in San Francisco there's no business like Joe business.)

Some time back there was a wave of Italian-restaurant closings along Broadway and upper Grant Avenue, as traditions were smothered by sleaze. The overflowing of Chinatown also changed the neighborhood. In the last few years, things seem to have stabilized, and there are some signs of a renewal—small ones perhaps, but evidence that it's premature to compose an elegy for the passing of North Beach.

A few notes: There tends to be a dichotomy in menus in North Beach; lunches are often much more Italianate than dinners, and you will find more deep-down specialties in many of the restaurants at midday, when locals and third-generation suburbanites who work in the city and cherish their memories gather for baccala, polenta, osso buco, and the like.

Given the number of family-style restaurants—where a four- or five-course meal is standard for a fixed price—and the number of modified multi-course meals, here are our criteria for price scales: a three-to-five course meal for under eight dollars is inexpensive; an entrée for the same price including a choice of soup or salad, with reasonably priced appetizers, is moderate; anything above that is expensive. In some cases, the high quality of the food is such that an "expensive" meal ranks as a relative bargain, and I have indicated those.

ADOLPH'S

641 Vallejo (between Stockton and Columbus)
392-6333

With an unassuming facade, on an even more unassuming block, Adolph's has two strikes against it from the start, but the kitchen hits a home run—this is a serious restaurant, and a real find.

Adolph Motta was one of those dedicated souls who seem to live in their restaurants. Like many of the other immigrants who made North Beach what it is, he thrived on the Old World virtues of hard work and fierce loyalty—many of the staff have been there for years.

At some point in the last decade, the restaurant seemed to have fallen from favor; old-timers stopped recommending it. Then Adolph sold the place to chef Alberto Mourino and one of his waiters, Paolo Carboni, and they proceeded to put some snap back into the place.

They kept the menu, with its wooden language and charming misspellings, and they kept the staff; what seems to have been added is a sense of pride.

You enter through the bar, which immediately feels like a trattoria—simple, functional, warm, with wine bottles everywhere, an integral part of the decor. The bar is crowned by a brass espresso machine which is a work of art in itself.

The dining room is dominated by a large mural and of course more wine bottles in every available nook and cranny; fresh flowers are on every white-linened table.

The menu abounds in veal, chicken, and fish dishes, not well described; if you didn't know about the first-rate kitchen, it would even seem like a collection of Italian clichés, which makes the revelations that follow even more fun.

There is a selection of complete dinners, reasonably priced, representing a cross-section of the menu, and a good set of bargains, all things considered.

There are a number of specialties, however, that yield delights of a much higher order: among the pasta dishes, the misnamed *Capellini Flambé* and *Linguine with White Clam Sauce*. Capellini is the thinnest spaghetti you can get, very hard to cook *al dente*; here, they begin cooking it in the kitchen and finish it sautéed at tableside, so it's just right, served with a thick, rich meat sauce. The linguine is also *al dente*, and the clam sauce doesn't fool around.

Among the entrées there are two outstanding specialties of the house, similarly under-described: *Capon* and either *Petrale* or *Red Snapper Mediterraneo*. The capon is actually a boned breast of chicken stuffed with veal, prosciutto, mozzarella cheese, and herbs, rolled in flavored bread crumbs and almond slivers, and baked; it comes accompanied by a mushroom sauce so thick and rich it qualifies as a vegetable course. The fish is either petrale or red snapper— whichever is freshest that day—lightly sautéed in a shallot-butter-lemon sauce, then baked with hearts of palm and whatever vegetables strike the chef's fancy at the moment.

Another option is *Gamberoni*, prawns sautéed with garlic, lemon, butter, and fresh tomatoes.

The *Zabaglione* is in the classic style, and of course the espresso machine provides either espresso or cappuccino.

The service, as might be expected when one is being taken care of by the owners, is quite attentive.

The wine list is very good, featuring some outstanding California wines and very good Italians. Vintages aren't listed, but be assured that some of the best of California's recent years are among them, and a few are a steal.

Adolph's is open seven days a week for dinner only, from 5:30 PM to midnight on weekdays, and 5:30 PM to 1:00 AM on weekends. Prices are moderate to expensive. Reservations are advised, major credit cards accepted. There is full bar service and free parking.

ALFRED'S

886 Broadway
781-7058

Alfred's sits above the Broadway tunnel, overlooking the neon and noise of the strip below, and perhaps too often overlooked by San Franciscans who have forgotten that it is one of the city's best steakhouses, with a touch of Italianate flair.

The restaurant was founded in 1928 by Alfred Bacchini, and featured corn-fed steaks shipped directly from Chicago's Union Stockyards. Several well-known North Beach chefs were trained there, and attest to Signor Bacchini's high standards; six years ago the restaurant was purchased by Arthur and Al Petri, who are maintaining them.

The restaurant is all comfortable, old-fashioned elegance—dark red walls, huge ring chandeliers overhead, fresh flowers on every table. The atmosphere is formal without being stuffy.

The keynote is still corn-fed Eastern beef, and although the menu features a number of Italian dishes which are well prepared, the steak is too good to skip. There is a good range of à la carte appetizers, salads, and pastas, but the best way to dine here is to order a full dinner for an extra four dollars and get a bit of everything.

Alfred's Celebrated Antipasto should be—it salvages the increasingly lost art of creating something unique for a first course. This antipasto features pickled pigs' feet, calamari vinaigrette, a kidney-bean salad, green and black olives, raw vegetable sticks, and slices of salami, coppa, and mortadella. This is followed by a choice of pasta or soup. Of the pastas, the ravioli, generously filled and spicy, is best, and the meat sauce covering it is honest and hearty. Soups are very good, obviously made from scratch. This course is followed by a mixed green salad with a good oil-vinegar-and-mustard house dressing.

Then comes the steak. Two cuts, *Filet Mignon* and *New York*, can be ordered in two sizes for those who choose to be sensible about the whole business; the smaller cuts are perfectly adequate, the normal sizes gargantuan. The rarely-seen *Delmonico Steak* is also featured, and highly recommended.

All the steaks are broiled over Mexican mesquite charcoal, crisply seared on the outside and juicy and tender inside, with a flavor that indicates not only corn-feeding but coddling and pampering. They are as thick as they ought to be. The meat comes with another rarity, a real baked potato, not some mushy thing steamed in aluminum foil. Green vegetables with an Italian accent, such as chard or zucchini, are also featured.

One other dish—also from the broiler—should be mentioned: *Rack of Lamb*, among the best in the city.

The wine list features a number of good selections from Italy, California, and France; the California wines are especially well chosen. The prices are gratifyingly reasonable, too.

The service is good. A number of the waiters have been at the restaurant for years, always a reassuring sign.

Lunch at Alfred's features a couple of Italian specials besides steaks, and they are well worth trying—especially *Osso Buco* or *Lamb Shanks*. However, the quality of the raw material, and the talent in the kitchen, pretty much guarantee that anything will be good.

Alfred's is open seven days a week for dinner, from 5:30 to 11:00 PM, and for lunch Monday through Friday from 12:00 to 2:30 PM. Prices are moderate to expensive. Reservations are advised, major credit cards accepted. There is full bar service, and valet parking.

AMELIO'S

1630 Powell Street (between Union and Green)
397-4339

Amelio's began in 1927 as a speakeasy and has gone through several incarnations. Most of the time, it's been a good Italian restaurant, in later years evolving into a fancy and expensive one. Today, the emphasis is mostly on Continental dishes, still fancy and expensive.

There are two dining rooms downstairs (the upstairs is a dining room for private parties); lighting is subdued, wallpaper red and plush, fixtures ornate, the feeling formal. Service is all from tableside carts—very good theater.

The menu is à la carte, and generally executed quite well all around. (At these prices, it better be!) Staying with our theme—and something they do especially well—try the *Fettuccine*, deftly finished at tableside with heaps of real, rich Parmesan cheese; *Veal Alfredo*, perhaps the best piccata in town, with a very light but intense sauce loaded with mushrooms; and *Raspberries Cassis*, a glass of fresh berries drenched in the liqueur, topped with fresh cream.

Service is excellent and solicitous. The wine list is extensive and expensive, with the markups more painful than they need or should be.

Amelio's is open for dinner only, from 5:30 PM to 10:30 PM seven nights a week. Expensive. Reservations recommended. Major credit cards accepted. Full bar service. Parking garage across the street.

CAFFE SPORT

574 Green Street (near Columbus)
981-1251

To begin with, Caffe Sport is a massive monument to Italian *kitsch*, an obsessive-compulsive endeavor that begins to rival the Watts Towers' mad accumulations. There is stuff everywhere, but not just plain stuff—this is no ordinary obsession, this is a wonderfully gaudy southern Italian obsession. It demands mirrors, brass and other shiny surfaces, an enormous model of a galleon painted in primary colors, collages of bright, unlikely materials, borders of pinto beans trapped under resined tabletops . . . in short, a glorious madness.

And it is good that there is so much to see, because you will have plenty of time to look.

Here is how it goes: There are two seatings a night, at 6:30 and 8:30. Reservations are necessary and they fill up early, so you should start calling a little before 11:00 AM. The line will be busy; you have to keep trying. If you get through early enough, you may get the first seating. If you can't get through, the next best idea is to go there for lunch and make your reservation in person.

Arrive early for dinner. The place begins to fill up around six, no one seems sure what is going on, and mass hysteria slowly settles in. At 6:35, nothing is happening yet, and the middle of the growing crowd is not a good place to be. At 6:40, a waiter who sounds and acts like Chico Marx appears with a rough chart showing names and places. Despite this, a lot of shuffling goes on until everyone is seated, with a great deal of banter filling the air, not all of it humorous.

Sitting down feels like a small victory; you think that you're past the worst hurdle, but they're just fooling you. There is a menu for each table, and if you are at one of the large tables it may be a while before it gets to you. You are asked if you want wine, white or red. By now you know enough not to ask what it is, or for a list; you call out a color and size, and a carafe is plunked down after a while. The house red is the worst in North Beach.

Plates, silverware, napkins are thrust upon you. Bread arrives, and if you are lucky you may get butter. By now the customers have been here for more than an hour, drinking beer or wine, and they are beginning to make as much noise as the waiters. At this point, a few non-Mediterraneans usually give up and walk out.

Ordering makes you aware of what you are really involved in here: an Italian Mad Hatter's Tea Party. You order one of the many pasta dishes, say *Pasta alle Vongole*; the waiter doesn't write anything down. What else you gonna have? You order *Prawns*. He recommends another kind of pasta, like *con Pesto*. You insist on the other pasta, he shakes his head. You insist again, and he smiles: We're out of that. Gotcha! You capitulate, of course. He goes away. You make friends with your neighbors. The bread is all gone. So are the waiters. A moment before bleak and utter despair sets in, they reappear, arms laden with platters, and the aroma of garlic fills the air.

By now, after all this, you are saying that it had better be good.

It is. Really good. The prawns are jumbo-sized, and there are plenty of them, swathed in olive oil and garlic creamed together with a bit of parsley, atop a layer of *al dente* zucchini. The pasta the waiter chose is indeed the best partner for the prawns. Everyone goes into a feeding frenzy, like sharks.

The noise level now rises and your view is blocked. It is all the people who are here for the 8:30 seating, watching you eat, their anxiety palpable. You feel like Marie Antoinette with a conscience; you'd throw them scraps of bread if there were any left. You pay the check and flee.

You've had an experience, and you've eaten good food, but you haven't had a *dining* experience, you've had the Caffe Sport experience.

Would you go back? The food is as good as you can get in North Beach, especially if you like garlic. And now you know the routine, and how to fight back. Perhaps you will round up half a dozen friends (so that you can try for a table all to yourselves) and make an amiable frontal assault on the place, roll with the punches, take your lumps, and enjoy the show and the food. You may even kid the waiter this time. You might as well . . . .

Caffe Sport is open Tuesday through Saturday, with a light lunch (great calamari) from 11:30 AM to 2:30 PM, and dinner as stated above. Prices are somewhat expensive; major credit cards are accepted. Bar service consists of beer and wine only.

CAFFERATA RAVIOLI FACTORY

700 Columbus Avenue (at Filbert)
392-7544

Nothing Italian is ever simple, so it's eminently logical that the Cafferata Ravioli Factory is several things more than just that; it is also a source of other kinds of fresh pasta, a delicatessen, and a restaurant.

Once you get past the drab and dingy facade, it's quite pleasant and even airy inside, thanks to the high ceiling, white walls, and sunlight flooding in from several sides. The floor is white tile, and the chairs are metal folding types, but a touch of cheer is supplied by the red-checked oilcloths on the tables.

Along one wall is the deli case, with a wide variety of meats and cheeses, and salamis hanging overhead. Tucked away on the other side of the opposite wall is the pasta manufactory. When a pasta customer comes in, one of the waitresses chats for a moment about types of pasta and how many are to be served and goes and gets the right amount; cooking advice is freely dispensed. (Hot prepared food is also available to take out.)

The menu for lunch consists of a variety of pastas in either cheese or tomato sauce; most are executed quite well. The *Cheese Ravioli* is especially good, with a healthy amount of basil in with the cheese. *Tortellini* is also very good, with either sauce. Sandwiches are available, as are things like *Lasagna*. All meals come with generous amounts of good bread and butter. The dinner menu is the same, with the addition of a couple of meat entrées such as *Veal Marsala*.

There is no jukebox, and the only diversion is the people walking by outside, glimpsed through the multitude of plants in the windows. Much of the clientele is Italian, so there is usually a musical murmur of that language in the background. Altogether, this is a very pleasant place for a light lunch.

The service is casual and friendly. Beer and wine are available; the house wine is decent and reasonably priced, and there are some imported bottles available on request.

Cafferata Ravioli Factory is open Monday through Saturday for lunch from 11:00 AM to 3:00 PM. Dinners are served Wednesday through Saturday from 5:00 PM to 10:00 PM, and on Sundays from 3:00 PM to 10:00 PM. Prices are inexpensive to moderate. No reservations. MasterCard and Visa accepted. Beer and wine only. Parking garage across the street.

CAPP'S CORNER

1600 Powell Street (at the corner of Powell and Green)
989-2589

As you step into Capp's, you are immediately aware that Joe Capp has a lot of friends—the walls are lined with hundreds of color photos of them, frequently out-of-focus, in a quite goofy montage that sums the place up perfectly. The clientele is a perfect cross-section of North Beach: The audience is also the show. If the jukebox is going, you will be tossed back in time to when people fox-trotted to Jerry Vale and Sinatra, and the dim lighting is an asset.

Capp's has family-style service, although there are a number of small tables available. The menu lists five entrées only: usually chicken, veal, fish, beef or a stew, and corned beef and cabbage. The kitchen is not consistent, and chicken, fish and stew are best choices—especially stew, since stocks and sauces tend to be pretty good here.

You begin with soup, frequently a thick, complicated *minestrone*, with various vegetables and pasta in there; the accompanying sourdough bread is good too. Salad follows, very plain, just lettuce and kidney and garbanzo beans. A heaping plate of pasta with meat sauce is next, its chief virtue being its abundance.

Then the entrée. If you order veal, you might get slightly over-cooked slices of meat in a wonderful lemon-butter-capers-and-something-else sauce. The various versions of chicken are better. All are accompanied by a green vegetable and a scoop of mashed potatoes, which at this point seems thoroughly unnecessary.

Dessert (good spumoni) and coffee are included, so at under eight dollars, dinner at Capp's has to be something of a bargain. The house wine is the estimable North Beach favorite, Rege, and there is a small selection (which the waitress will recite) of reasonably priced wines. including a number of half-bottles.

The service is notably good—quick, alert, and friendly. On most nights, the bar is presided over by the legendary Hal Thunes, another good reason to stop in.

Capp's Corner is open seven days a week, with lunch from 11:30 AM to 2:30 PM and dinner from 5:00 to 10:00 PM. Major credit cards are accepted, and there is full bar service. A parking garage is across the street.

FIOR D'ITALIA

621 Union Street (at Stockton)
986-1886

The "Flower of Italy" is San Francisco's oldest Italian restaurant and, after some ups and downs, again one of the best. It opened on May 15, 1886, and was run by the same family until just recently, without a break in its operation.

The first incarnation was a hole-in-the-wall on Broadway near Jackson, on the border of what was then the notoriously rowdy Barbary Coast. A few years later, seeking more room and perhaps a bit more peace and quiet, the Marionetti family moved down the street, close to Columbus Avenue. The move was accomplished between the time the restaurant closed after dinner and the time it opened for breakfast in the new location (which is now, by the way, Enrico's).

The record of continuous service was preserved during the Great Earthquake in 1906, which reduced the building to an untidy heap of rubble. With a kind of stoic opportunism, the Marionettis built a fire and made kettles of minestrone, and within a week were running the restaurant out of a tent.

In 1954, perhaps anticipating the topless-bottomless seediness that soon prevailed on Broadway, Frank and George Marionetti moved up the street and around the corner to the present location, on Washington Square facing the church of Saints Peter and Paul. The menu then was impressively long and varied; it was a first-class restaurant.

With time, the flower faded; age caught up with the owners, the building, and the kitchen equipment. Old-timers spoke of Fior d'Italia only with regret.

In 1977, a group of Italian-American businessmen, all native San Franciscans, bought the place and completely renovated and expanded it, buying a store next door which was opened into a handsome bar and informal dining room. Most important, they installed an ultramodern kitchen and a first-rate chef and cooks.

The building takes up half the block between Stockton and Columbus, and from the time you step in the door, there is no doubt as to the restaurant's orientation. The long oak bar, bentwood chairs, and tile floors are pure old San Francisco-saloon-style, while the oversized windows down the other wall illuminate an enormous mural of the seven hills of Rome. This room, with its view of Washington Square and the church, is a favorite place for lunch.

Inside, the lighting is subdued, the atmosphere that of a very plush Italian terrace. There's a small fountain and pool, there are statues discreetly placed, flowers everywhere, and Italian songs and opera playing quietly in the background. Half-partitions maintain the open feeling but insure an intimate aspect at the same time, and this is reinforced by thick carpeting that helps keep the noise level low.

The food is predominantly northern Italian, the sauces generally light and natural. Some of the specialities are original, such as *Veal Stelvio*, named after the chef, and *Chicken Mascotte*. The veal dish is thin cutlets of excellent, milk-fed veal sautéed with mushrooms and white wine, and garnished with thin shreds of prosciutto; the chicken is half a bird, sautéed, then browned in the oven, and capped with mushrooms and artichokes in an aromatic wine-and-shallot sauce.

Minestrone is always a good indication of the seriousness of an Italian restaurant, and the thick soup here is obviously home-made, long-simmered, and from an original recipe—it's just a little different from most, and terrific.

Another unusual dish is *Chicken Valdostana*, boneless chicken breast stuffed with mozzarella cheese; the cheese melts just enough to stick to the chicken, not enough to be messy or stringy.

Fior also serves the best *gnocchi* in town. Done right, these little featherweight puffs are like nothing you've ever had, and here they are done right.

If you somehow have room for dessert after sampling all that should be tried, then your best shot is the *Zabaglione Montecarlo*. There are as many variations on this classic as there are restaurants in the world, and Fior's is right up there with the best of them. Another plus at this point in the meal is well-made espresso.

The wine list is extensive and reasonably priced. Of course, it's heavy on Italian wines, but California is well represented too; most importantly, the wines are chosen with care—no second-rate choices here.

The bar is also a nice place to stop and just have a drink; it's generally reasonably quiet and quite comfortable, and between 5 PM and 7 PM baskets of hot and crispy *calamari fritti* are served which make all other appetizers seem trivial by comparison.

Fior d'Italia is open seven days a week, from 11 AM to 11 PM. The prices are moderate to expensive. (Bear in mind that the menu is all à la carte.) There is full bar service, reservations are recommended, all major credit cards are accepted, and there is valet parking.

GOLD SPIKE

527 Columbus Avenue (between Union and Green)
986-9747

The Gold Spike dates back more than fifty years, but looking around, you'd swear it was at least one hundred. The walls are a hodgepodge of American, Californian, and Italian artifacts and pictures, with thousands of business cards tacked onto or tucked into every piece. Deer heads with Chianti bottles hanging from the antlers; postcards, paintings, and posters; gold pans and picks—there are too many pieces to enumerate. The total effect is a little crazy, and quite wonderful, especially now that the macaw that used to imitate a cat and sometimes swear has died.

The facade of the place is the most unassuming in North Beach—two storefronts side by side, with windows painted an ugly ochre up past eye level and offering no hint of what to expect behind them. Inside are a bar/dining area with banquettes along the walls, and a second dining room (next door). The tables are set with red-checked oilcloth, and there is a jukebox heavy on favorites from the Fifties and Sixties, in case you need more entertainment than the walls provide.

Dinner begins with a thin but spicy minestrone, peppery and containing quite a few different vegetables. An antipasto of sliced salami, hot peppers, and sweet pickles arrives at the same time, as does sourdough bread and lots of butter. Then comes a salad—lettuce, pickled beets, minced carrot, and tomatoes, with a bowl of kidney beans on the side, as a garnish.

Now comes a plate of pasta, usually ravioli and rigatoni in a slightly bland but meaty sauce; there is a jar of grated cheese on the table, and the ravioli is quite good.

The best way to pace yourself through all this, by the way, is to hold off on deciding what your entrée will be until about this point in the meal. This buys you a little time to breathe, relax, decide what sort of diet you're going on tomorrow. . . .

There are usually five entrées to choose from: a couple of beef dishes, a veal, a chicken, maybe two. The *Chicken Cacciatore* is good, as are *Sirloin Tips alla Romana* and *Roast Beef*. One redeeming feature of many of the dishes are the sauces, which tend to be spicy without knocking you off your chair. All dishes are accompanied by a potato and a green vegetable. As a number of things here are cooked ahead, dining earlier means dining better.

Dessert is spumoni, and coffee is included.

The service is friendly, even motherly, but quite efficient. There are a variety of wines available, but the house wines are inexpensive and good: a bargain.

During winter and early spring, on Friday nights, the Gold Spike serves a killer *cioppino*, a testament to the glory of fresh crabs, messy and abundant and absolutely wonderful.

The Gold Spike is open from 5:00 PM to 10:00 PM, Thursday through Tuesday. Prices are inexpensive. No reservations, no credit cards. There is full bar service.

GREEN VALLEY

510 Green Street (between Grant and Columbus)
788-9384

The Green Valley is at either the beginning or the end of the line, geographically speaking, of the family-style restaurants on Green Street. It is the personification of drabness inside and out, and is utterly lacking in charm, but it does offer some fine values.

You enter through the bar, which could not be plainer; the adjoining dining room possesses a checked linoleum floor, dark furniture, a rather ugly large painting, and an equally large poster for Italian wine, thoroughly overblown. The subdued lighting helps a great deal. The wine glasses are three-ounce shot glasses, napkins are skimpy paper, and the silverware almost matches. If business is slow, the chef is liable to stop chatting with customers and seat you and run through the menu with you.

There are a number of entrées to choose from, of which we can recommend *Boiled Beef* and *Roast Beef*. The former comes with "vinaigrette" sauce, which is a puréed mixture of onions, garlic, olive oil, parsley, and capers, altogether pungent and quite assertive—and terrific. The complete dinner here is under eight dollars; for two dollars more you can get *New York Steak*, and it is highly recommended, as (for one dollar extra) are *Lamb Chops* in an old-fashioned thick version. Be firm about the degree of doneness, though.

The meal starts with either a plain salad or a fairly vapid minestrone (which sometimes includes lentils, oddly enough). There are three kinds of pasta to choose from, and they all come *al dente* or close to it; the best is *Pasta al Pesto*, which has the best oil-based pesto sauce in town, classic in its simplicity: chopped basil (a lot of it), garlic, and olive oil mixed together, adorned with a pat of butter. There is nothing at all understated about this version. After all this, spumoni and coffee are included in the meal.

Most of the wine available is Italian, though there are a few Californiania wines offered. Prices are quite reasonable. Service is offhand, but friendly.

Green Valley is open from 11:30 AM to 2:30 PM for lunch and from shortly thereafter until 1:00 PM for dinner; closed Tuesdays. Major credit cards accepted, reservations not necessary. Full bar service.

GUIDO'S

347 Columbus Avenue (between Vallejo and Broadway)
982-2157

There are frequently long lines outside of Guido's, which is not an easy phenomenon to understand. Not that there's anything wrong with the place—in fact quite the oppostie—but there is also nothing particularly special about it, either.

Like so many other places along this part of Columbus, Guido's has odd angles and is shallow, but comfortable. Natural wood, wine bottles, and pink linens give it a soft, warm feeling which is a triumph of decor over angularity. Fresh flowers and candles help a great deal.

The menu is brief, with the French dishes just edged out by the Italian ones; the French influence does extend to several of the sauces, however—too much and too floury.

There are a number of redeeming factors. *Fettuccine with Cream Cheese Sauce* is nicely understated and light, and is served *al dente*. A basket of hot sourdough toasted with Romano cheese is a delightful extra, as is the small plate of *French Fried Zucchini*: thick sticks dipped in batter and lightly fried, crisp on the outside and just cooked inside. Salad, which also comes with the dinner, is plain butter lettuce with a good house dressing.

Veal here is cut thick, but the meat is tender enough, with good flavor. *Veal Guido* comes drenched in a white mustard sauce with plenty of mushrooms, and *Veal Scaloppine* features a tomato-eggplant-mushroom sauce that is very good. Two vegetables are served, one of them frequently a summer squash topped with a light tomato-based sauce.

The wine list is mediocre and slightly overpriced. Service is attentive, but can get somewhat laggard on busy nights.

Guido's is open for dinner only, Tuesday through Saturday, from 6:00 PM to 11:00 PM. Reservations recommended. Major credit cards accepted. Beer and wine only. Slightly expensive.

IL GIGLIO

545 Francisco (between Mason and Taylor)
441-1040

"The Lily" is a jewel box of a restaurant, small and elegant and relatively new by North Beach standards—it's only been open since 1970. However, its owner and sometime chef, Lorenzo Picchi, has been cooking his way through North Beach for many years.

Chef Picchi's family emigrated here right after World War II. In the classic fashion, they remade their lives from the ground up—the boy Lorenzo and his father went to work as busboys at New Joe's, and both ended up owning their own restaurants.

At one point, he put in three years cooking under Roger Bertolla, one of the great chefs of San Francisco and, according to Lorenzo, one of the great teachers as well, always experimenting with variations on recipes and encouraging his staff to do the same.

In 1970, Lorenzo sold a restaurant in order to create one from scratch, gutting an industrial building to the walls and setting up everything just as he wished. (The kitchen is a marvel—clean, roomy, and organized for efficiency.)

The small dining room (it seats forty-four) immediately informs you that they are not fooling around at Il Giglio. The walls are warm pink and gold, bearing antique mirrors and crystal lights; the linen is a lovely peach color; and a large chandelier reigns imposingly over all, casting the right amount of light to enhance the setting and preserve the intimate feeling.

The food here is predominantly northern Italian, with the emphasis on veal; no oil is used in the preparation of the food—the sauces are butter- or wine-based—so the dishes tend to be somehow rich and light at the same time. The pasta is made on the premises, and the herbs are always fresh.

Two of Chef Picchi's original dishes are best to begin with for appetizers: *Shrimp Etruscan* or *Asparagi della Casa*. The former (which also comes in a crab version when crabs are in season) is tiny Bay shrimp, lightly sautéed with bread crumbs, six herbs, and grated Parmesan cheese, and served in scallop shells; the latter is stalks of white asparagus, lightly browned in butter and sprinkled with paprika and Parmesan.

THE FLAVOR OF NORTH BEACH

The pasta is outstanding. Something different to try is *Tortellini*, little twisted rolls of pasta stuffed with chopped meat and spices, napped in a rich and creamy sauce.

In the veal department, two dishes which are slightly different are the lemon version, in which the veal is lightly sautéed in a simple butter-and-lemon sauce, and *Vitello alla Giglio*, with a sauce of wine, butter, and slivered almonds. Fresh fish and some interesting chicken dishes fill out the menu, which is all à la carte.

The best desserts at Il Giglio are based on fresh fruits—for example, strawberries rolled in brown sugar and covered with cream which is laced with brandy and Grand Marnier. There is also espresso, of course.

The wine list highlights California and Italian wines, decent choices at decent prices, nothing extraordinary but nothing bad, either. There is no bar or liquor service.

Lunch is one of the better bargains in town, as they serve the appetizers we've mentioned, plus the pasta of the day, an entrée, dessert, and coffee. (The portions are mercifully scaled down a little from the size of the dinner portions.) The same care in preparation and attentive service prevail.

Il Giglio is open Monday through Saturday, from 11:30 AM to 2 PM for lunch and from 5:30 PM to 11:30 PM for dinner. The prices range from moderate to expensive. Reservations are essential, major credit cards accepted; there is no valet parking, but there is a watchful doorman.

JOVANELO'S

840 Sansome Street (at Broadway)
986-8050

Jovanelo's opened almost ten years ago, the ornate creation of Joe and
Nello Piccinini (they are not related), who had paid their dues in a
variety of ways: Nello has worked all over town from swamper up to
maitre d', and looks far too young to remember North Beach in the
Thirties, while Joe learned to cook under the best chefs on Broadway
when he immigrated from Lucca in the mid-Forties.

There is a tiny bar up front which opens onto a fairly large dining
room, partitioned so that it retains a very cozy feeling wherever you
are. The room is slightly underlit. Dark red is the dominant color,
brass lamps and large, lush oil paintings adorn the walls, and the total
effect is one of being in the best turn-of-the-century *bagnio* in town.

The menu is extensive and impressive. The complete-dinner menu
offers the best highlights of what is done here, and is something of a
bargain to boot.

It begins with antipasto, and there is a lot of it: slices of mortadella
and salami, green and black olives, kidney-and-garbanzo-bean salad,
flaky red tuna in olive oil, and pickled vegetables. It's best to go easy.

Next comes an authoritative minestrone, thick and sturdy, with just
enough pasta in it. A good green salad is an alternative for the timid.

Then, a light, crêpe-like *Cannelloni*, filled with a mix of chicken and
veal, and smothered in a white sauce flavored with nutmeg, white
pepper, and ricotta and provolone cheeses.

After all this, light entrées are called for, and two of the best are the
offbeat *Chicken Jerusalem* and the *Scampi*. The chicken is cooked with a
white sauce incorporating baby artichokes and mushrooms, while the
scampi is langoustina in butter and garlic, with a definite statement
made by the latter. Sliced, sautéed potatoes and a green vegetable
accompany them. Another good choice is *Veal alla Palermo*, slathered
with green peppers and tomato sauce, thoroughly Sicilian.

If by any chance you can make room for dessert, try the *Rum Cake*
and a cup of excellent espresso.

The wine list is surprisingly unimaginative—made up of the same
kind of old-fashioned, middle-of-the-road selections you see all over
North Beach—but at least it's reasonably priced, and there are some
good wines listed. Service is quite good.

Jovanelo's is open Monday through Friday for lunch, from 11:30 AM
to 3:00 PM, and for dinner seven days a week, from 5:30 to 10:00,

although the small bar is open later. Prices are moderate to expensive. Reservations are advised, major credit cards accepted. Full bar service, valet parking.

LA BUSSOLA

800 Greenwich Street (between Mason and Columbus)
776-9161

"The Compass" is an unassuming place always in danger of being lost, located as it is on a sliver of a block, with only a narrow facade showing to busy Columbus Avenue. But it's worth seeking out, for several reasons. For one thing, the basic fare here is Sicilian-style food, which is rare in North Beach; for another, it's a cellar, rather romantic, with every cliché of such places proudly displayed for your amusement.

There are fresh flowers on every table, red tablecloths, wine bottles artfully displayed, and candles. A light clutter of objects hangs from the ceiling, and the plaster has been carefully chipped away from the walls to expose brick. Near the back of the restaurant, there are semi-private dining rooms for large parties.

The menu offers a variety of dishes, with veal and chicken predominating; all are rendered just that much different by the no-nonsense sauces. Minestrone or salad is included with the meal, and given the size of the portions, salad is the best choice—it's simple, with a good, tart oil-and-vinegar herb dressing. Hot bread is also served.

There is a good selection of pastas (these are extra), and they are happy to split orders. A good choice is *Tagliarini alla Bussola*, with bay shrimp and clams in a sauce of tomato, garlic, parsley, and other spices—very assertive.

Chicken Cacciatore is perhaps the best of the chicken offerings, richly sauced with tomatoes and peppers and garlic, not the usual rendition, and very good. *Italian Seafood Soup* is a house specialty, unlike any other in North Beach, and a personal favorite. "Soup" may be a misnomer, since the deep dish gets so filled with (from the bottom up) a thick slice of sourdough bread, two filets of sole, ringlets of calamari, and four large prawns. All this is drenched in a thick, rich stock heavy on the tomatoes, onions, and garlic.

There is a good wine list, mostly Italian, reasonably priced. Service is prompt, informative, and courteous.

La Bussola is open Tuesday through Saturday from 6:00 PM to 11:00 PM. Prices are moderate. Major credit cards accepted, reservations recommended on weekends. Beer and wine only.

LA CONTADINA

1800 Mason Street (at Union)
982-5728

"The Countrywoman" is just up the side of Russian Hill, alongside
the cable-car tracks. It's justly famous for sandwiches, served on hot
foggaccio, but there's a lot more to it than that. There is real talent in
the kitchen.

The decor (if that's the right word for it) is a cheerful clutter of
large photographs, posters, kitchen utensils, beer and wine bottles,
and anything else to fill up the space; it all looks as if it has slowly
evolved to this point, and will continue to do so. The furniture continues the theme—heavy old oak tables and chairs, most of which
don't quite match. Fresh flowers are on every table, in Italian beer or
Pellegrino mineral-water bottles. A melange of Italian music is always
in the air, from Rossini to raucous pop. Somehow it all hangs
together, with an ingenuous and slightly nutty charm.

The menu is neither long nor impressive, but everything is well
prepared from scratch, and the sauces display touches of ingenuity.
The antipasto is simple but fresh—thin slices (and freshly cut) of
salami, mortadella, and cappicolla; pickled peppers, olives, and jack
cheese. Salads are similarly simple, fresh, and quite hearty; the house
oil-and-vinegar herb dressing is balanced and light.

Cannelloni here is unique. The mix of meat ground together
includes veal, some cappicolla, a bit of salami, and apparently whatever else strikes the cook's fancy that day. Needless to say, it is spicy,
rich, and just unevenly textured enough to keep you alert. The sauce
is a good bechamel with a touch of nutmeg, some ricotta cheese
stirred in, and dollops of sharp tomato sauce around the edges. As
with the decor, it is odd but comes together nicely.

Pastas are good here, too, if you are firm about having them *al
dente*. Try the *Fettuccine al Pesto*, an unencumbered version featuring
nothing more than lots of basil, butter, and garlic, or the *Fettuccine
with Clam Sauce*, made with fresh clams.

The bread basket features sourdough and focaccia, which is studded
with bits of scallion and laced with garlic.

La Contadina does a heavy business with sandwiches to go, which is why not everyone knows about the excellence of the kitchen. The sandwiches are all hearty, and good, but the winner has to be the *Bella Burger*, a charbroiled hamburger on toasty focaccia which has been smeared on the inside with tomato sauce; add a slice of fresh tomato and onion, and you are on your way to heaven.

The wine list tilts heavily toward Italian wines, and offers middle-of-the-road selections at what seem to be fair prices. Peroni beer is featured, a light but malty Italian brew. The service is good, and friendly to boot.

La Contadina is open Tuesday through Saturday, from 11:30 AM to 3:30 PM for lunch and from 5:30 to 10:00 PM for dinner. Prices are moderate. No reservations, major credit cards accepted. Wine and beer only.

LA FELCE

1570 Stockton Street (at Union)
392-8321

"The Fern" has one of the most unassuming facades in North Beach, and has a stark and cheerless bar area; beyond them, however, is a cozy and cheerful dining room and a first-rate kitchen.

Liliano Salvetti, the chef and co-owner, is thoroughly Italian and has been cooking around North Beach for years. In 1974 he and Romano Marcucci bought the place and revived it, first as a family-style operation, now with a more formal menu. Marcucci tends bar, and his cheerfulness somewhat moderates the starkness of the bar. If you linger there, try the jukebox, which is full of Italian songs and what we think of as Italo-American oldies. (If you remember Jerry Vale, you understand.)

The menu combines the familiar with the unique, perhaps reflecting Chef Salvetti's variegated background. Two dishes, both very good but just a bit different from the usual, serve notice of this immediately. Start with either *Fettuccine al Pesto* or *Gnocchi Verdi*; both come napped in a creamy pesto sauce, rather than the plainer normal version, but it works.

Chicken Sauté Sec comes out quite brown on the outside and quite tender inside, and is a fine version of this old favorite. It's covered with fresh mushrooms and redolent of the white wine, rosemary, and garlic it was sautéed in.

Chicken Doré is a chicken breast pounded out, lightly battered with a flour-egg mixture, and sautéed in lemon and butter, ending up somehow light and rich at the same time. *Vitello il Ferri*, "veal by iron" more or less, is another pleasant surprise. A nice piece of veal is butterflied out to a wide, thin rectangle, pounded with pepper, salt, garlic, and a little oil, then quickly grilled so that the outside is seared and the inside remains tender. It is as simple and obvious as a paper clip, and why didn't we think of it?

All the entrées come with a healthy serving of a green vegetable, which makes for a nice guilt-free experience if you've begun with a pasta course.

At lunchtime, La Felce reverts to Old North Beach with a variety of dishes which only appear periodically in the evening as specials: *Osso Buco, Braciole, Baccala with Polenta, Roast Veal*, and much more, all herbed, spiced, and served up *con brio*.

The wine list is simple, straightforward, somewhat limited, and reasonably priced, with a balance between Italian and California selections—nothing bad, nothing great.

The service is good, attentive, alert, and informative.

La Felce is open Monday, Wednesday, Thursday and Friday for lunch from 11:30 AM to 2:00 PM, and from Wednesday to Monday, from 5:30 to 10:00 PM for dinner; closed all day Tuesday. Prices are moderate. Reservations are advised, major credit cards accepted. There is full bar service, and valet parking.

LA PANTERA

1234 Grant Avenue (between Columbus and Vallejo)
392-0170

"The Panther" was established right after the Earthquake, in 1907,
and hasn't changed much. The floor is worn white tile; the tables are
marble, the buff walls stamped tin, and the lights always bright. The
effect is quite cheery, enhanced by the groups of people at tables for
eight getting to know each other. This is probably the best example of
family-style dining left in North Beach.

The Nicolai family owned the place for many years, but it was
recently sold and there were fears that things would change. Those
fears were laid to rest when Rena Nicolai, who runs the dining room
like an amiable drillmaster, stayed on, insuring the continuity
of custom.

Dinners are under nine dollars, which includes the small bottle of
rough red wine at each setting. You start with a mini-antipasto of
salami and olives, then go on to homemade soup, which might be
split pea or minestrone or something else, but which is always hearty.
Then comes a pasta course, usually drenched in a plain but sharp
tomato sauce, sometimes pesto. (Part of the get-acquainted process at
La Pantera involves passing around the plates.)

There is a choice of two entrées every night, and they can be a little
uneven. *Veal Stew* is always good, as is *Roast Chicken*; the former is
spicy and thick, the latter rubbed with garlic and oil, and crisply
browned. *Sole* is sautéed in a light batter, and highly recommended. A
green vegetable accompanies it.

Next comes a salad: crisp torn lettuce with carrot curls and
garbanzo and kidney beans. Cruets of oil and vinegar accompany it,
and you mix your own dressing. Then a plate of fresh fruit and slices
of cheese arrives. A good way to complete the experience is to amble
up to the bar for a coffee-cognac and catch Reggie, the owner-
bartender, putting on his own show, kidding Mrs. Nicolai and
the customers.

There is a selection of California and Italian wines, one of each type
(Cabernet Sauvignon, Barbera, Chianti, etc.), and reasonably priced.
The available wines are displayed atop a cabinet, which somehow fits
the casual ambience.

La Pantera is open from 6 PM to 10 PM Tuesday through Sunday.
Reservations are accepted only for eight or more. No credit cards. Full
bar service.

LA VERANDA

1433 Union Street (at Grant Street)
397-8831

La Veranda is utterly southern Italian in all its approaches—that is, quite laid-back. The service is slow, but warm and solicitous; the decor is sort of thrown together; the kitchen can't be rushed; and the food is abundant and spicy and heavy on the carbohydrates.

There are three pinball machines to occupy you while you wait for dinner, and a jukebox featuring an odd cross-section of music. All in all, the place is much like the quick-lunch joints that dot Italy's *autostradas*, not at all fancy but with their own kind of charmingly peculiar atmosphere.

The menu is a little bit of everything: antipasto and hearty sandwiches served with a bowl of minestrone; a couple of pasta courses; lasagna and cannelloni. The main staple is pizza, which is made with a medium-thick crust that has a bread-like lightness; nine combinations are offered. They are light on the tomato sauce and cheese and heavy on the other ingredients, making them less killing than such concoctions usually are, and more like great open-faced sandwiches. The ingredients are fresh and honest, and we leave the combinations to your personal tolerances.

Another rarity on the menu is *Calzone*, a favorite in New York's Little Italy but not seen much here. Dough is rolled out and filled with a variety of ingredients, folded back over flat, and then baked; cheese is always one of the ingredients, and this whole thing surely is a sin—hot, rich, chewy, and caloric. If you must have it (and you should), try the spinach-ricotta combination, or perhaps the cheese-prosciutto, or the ham-cheese; if you really want decadence, go for the carciofi-capers and let the artichokes, capers, and cheese fight for possession of your palate.

Beverages include red, white, or rosé house wine; vermouth; and coffees. A good choice would be wine with dinner and iced espresso afterward—very strong; it brings you back down to earth like a maiden aunt, firm but fair.

La Veranda is open from 4:00 PM to 2:00 AM seven days a week. Inexpensive. No reservations, no credit cards. Wine and beer only.

LITTLE JOE'S

325 Columbus Avenue (between Grant and Vallejo)
982-7639

Little Joe's is thought of by many people as the best counter restaurant
in North Beach. It cerainly seems to be the most popular. Certainly,
also, for the size of the place, it has the most ambitious menu, and the
execution is consistently good.

Little Joe's has been expanded, with a small dining room (Baby
Joe's) which you can step down into. Tables are crammed together,
and you can't help getting to know your neighbors, which is part of
the fun. Otherwise, if you want to eat at the counter, simply take up a
station along the wall behind someone who looks close to finishing—
the system here is either democracy or anarchy, depending on your
good humor. The rich mix of aromas is a powerful inducement to
your appetite.

Most people prefer to sit at the counter and watch the show, as the
cooks seem to handle three or four tasks at the same time, while singing,
joking, and yelling at each other. Baby Joe's is slightly less hectic.

There are nightly specials. Among the notable ones are *Filet of Sole*
(enormous amount, sautéed nicely), *Caciucco* (rich fish stew), *Chicken
Sauté with Polenta*, and a pungent *Stuffed Pepper*. All come with a
choice of vegetables, spaghetti, or rigatoni.

Among the regular entrées, two notable ones are *Boiled Beef* (thick
slices heavily garnished with what they merely call "vinaigrette,"
actually a cold *salsa verde* composed of finely chopped onions, parsley,
garlic, and capers), and *Spaghetti with Clams*, an enormous, plate-fill-
ing mound of pasta covered with a multitude of baby clams and thin
but garlic-spicy sauce; they should give a prize to anyone who can
finish it. There are many more pastas, omelettes, sandwiches, and
entrées, as Little Joe's tries to be all things to all people, and generally succeeds.

The wine list is reasonably priced, dominated by Italians. (The California selections are mainly Pellegrini, with deep roots in North
Beach.) There is a good beer selection, too. Service is quick, sometimes hectic, always cheerful.

Little Joe's is open from 11:00 AM to 7:30 PM Monday through
Saturday. Prices are inexpensive. No reservations, no credit cards. Beer
and wine only.

LUIGI'S

353 Columbus Avenue (between Vallejo and Broadway)
397-1697

Luigi's has been there for years, and is yet another Joe's-style place, long and narrow, with a counter on one side and naugahyde booths and formica tables on the other. The prices and the size of the portions have endeared the place to generations of students, artists, and other indigents.

The air is thick with the smells of everything being cooked. Spicy, smoky, even pungent, it is fair warning. There are two specials every night, one of which is usually Italian, the best of which may be *Chicken Parmigian*. There is a wide range of pastas (forget *al dente* here), most of which come with a sweet, thick tomato-meat sauce. Much of the menu is either short-order or steam table; therefore the service is notably quick.

The main reason to come here is to have a bottle of wine. They don't seem to sell much, so what you get is nicely aged: a half-bottle of Louis Martini Barbera, vintage 1974 (one of the best years ever in California), will set you back $3.75, and it is worth every penny. So are the other Californians available, so have a hamburger and fries with them and toast every beer-, coffee-, and soda-pop-drinker in the place who made it all possible.

Luigi's is open Wednesday through Monday, from 4:00 PM to 11:00 PM. Inexpensive, no reservations: Visa Card accepted. Beer and wine only.

NEW PISA

550 Green Street (between Grant and Columbus)
362-4726

The New Pisa and Dante Benedetti (they are synonymous) are North
Beach institutions. The restaurant moved to its present location only a
few years ago, but once Dante had covered the walls with fifty years'
worth of artifacts and pictures and filled the place with old friends, it
looked and felt as if it had always been right there.

The bar seems smaller than it is because of the clutter of sports
mementos all around the walls—pennants, posters, baseballs, trophies;
it's like a wonderful parody of a boy's bedroom, and perhaps deep
down it is. The television set is, however, rather small—Dante likes to
keep the business of drinking in perspective.

Through a small archway is the dining room, with booths and
tables along the walls and larger tables lengthwise down the middle. It
has the feeling of a real *galleria*, heightened by the noisily good-
natured crowd.

And why shouldn't they be happy? The food is good, just a little
different, abundant, and cheap.

Dining is family-style, five courses, and there are a lot of choices.
The salad is a large portion of lettuce, carrots, beets, two kinds of
beans, and sometimes slices of potato. *Minestrone* here is unique—not
so full-bodied, but with a beefy-peppery richness that really awakens
your tastebuds. The pasta of the day comes drenched in a spicy, oniony
sauce, and grated cheese is put before you in a bowl, for you to
partake of as you please.

Chicken Cacciatore also comes in a spicy sauce, but one which is not
too heavy, and it's well worth trying. Among the other dishes to
try here are *Roast Veal* and *Roast Chicken*—especially the veal—and
Osso Buco.

There is one unique dessert on the menu, well worth trying: *French
Bread Pudding*. It's slightly on the heavy side, but, infused with
cinammon, it's delightful; a tangy sauce which accompanies it, however, is really too much. Coffee comes with the meal.

The wine list is the usual limited selection of familiar names at quite
reasonable prices. Service is cheerful, friendly, and good.

New Pisa is open from 11:30 AM to 2:30 PM for lunch and from 2:30
PM to 11:00 PM for dinner every day but Wednesday. Prices are
inexpensive. No reservations, no credit cards. Full bar service.

NEW SAN REMO

2237 Mason Street (between Francisco and Chestnut)
673-9090

San Remo has been around for many years. For most of those years it was a thoroughly undistinguished place that attracted people more for the fact that it served large amounts of food at small prices than for anything to do with decor (drab) or quality (mediocre).

However, early in 1978 the restaurant was remodeled inside and out (it is a Victorian structure), a brand-new kitchen was installed, and an intriguing menu was set. The New San Remo blossomed.

The bar is long and the decor immediately announces that the owners have striven for the classic San Francisco saloon look, clean and open, with ceiling fans and etched glass mirrors. The dining room has low partitions topped by etched glass between its rows of tables, and these give it, too, an open look. Flowers abound, and dark carpeting keeps the noise low. It's all romantic and charming.

Dining here is sort of "family style," at least as that term is interpreted these days. Here, it means that you can order a complete dinner for a reasonable price—soup, salad, a pasta course, entrée, and dessert; just order the entrée and you put yourself in their hands. (You may also order à la carte, but that means really missing something. In a sense, the complete-dinner meals are a set of specials, changed around every day, and are well worth trying.)

The service is good, and the waiters and waitresses are very good about explaining things. Soup is made from scratch, lightly seasoned, usually hearty. The salad is generally just lettuce and purple onion tossed in an herb-oil-vinegar dressing. The type of pasta for the pasta course may vary, but comes with a meat sauce and a generous coating of grated cheese; the sauce is quite hearty and almost sweet somehow. Desserts tend to be on the simple side, the best being a good spumoni.

Among the entrées, there are a number of originals. Some of the better dishes are those based on thin-sliced, sautéed pork. *Pork Scaloppine* features slices of pork dipped in batter before being sautéed, then napped with a terrific, velvety brown sauce; *Pork Piccata* is sautéed in butter, lemon juice, and capers, like the veal version; *Pork Scaloppine Sorrentino* includes eggplant and mozzarella cheese.

Several of the chicken dishes also feature some original touches. *Chicken Lucas* is a plump breast covered with cheese, set into a nicely spiced bed of creamed spinach, and baked; all the flavors blend quite well into a whole greater than its parts. *Chicken Romana* features the same brown demi-glacé sauce as the *Pork Scaloppine*, with the addition of garlic and mushrooms.

The wine list is skimpy, with most wines merely named by types and no vintages listed. The actual wines offered are pretty good (though slightly overpriced), but a conversation with the server and even some trips to the kitchen may be necessary if you want to find out about the choices available. However, it is the policy of the house to mention, on the blackboard that announces the dinners of the day, a few special wines at reasonable prices. They are usually well chosen, and match the food offered.

The New San Remo is open seven days a week for dinner only, from 5:00 to 11:00 PM Monday through Saturday, and from 3:00 to 11:00 PM on Sunday. Prices are moderate. Reservations are advised, major credit cards accepted, full bar service offered.

NORTH BEACH RESTAURANT

1512 Stockton (at Columbus)
392-1700

The North Beach is run by two of the most colorful characters in the area (which is, of course, saying a lot). Bruno Orsi is the chef, and a very imaginative one; Lorenzo Petroni runs the dining room and the wine cellar, and sometimes directs traffic in front of the place.

Open only ten years, the North Beach has attracted a considerable following. Its several dining rooms and alcoves are frequently filled, but the intimate bar is a pleasant place to wait, especially if Lorenzo is holding forth there.

The wallpaper is deep red and the lighting is subdued. The waiters wear tuxedos, the menu is extensive, and the wine list is a book—this is a serious restaurant, no doubt about it.

One important thing about the place is unseen, and that is the sixty-foot fishing trawler which Signors Orsi and Petroni bought a few years ago. It guarantees them a good supply of fresh fish for the restaurant, and they barter with other fishermen when their catch is too heavy on any one type.

Chef Orsi is a master *saucier*, so many of the veal dishes here are a bit different from the versions with the same names you find elsewhere. He cures his own prosciutto, too, so any dish featuring that has an advantage going in.

He also makes his own pasta, and his *Spaghetti Carbonara* is as different and as good a spaghetti dish as you will find, lightly coated with cheese and laden with prosciutto. For those who prefer to deprive themselves of pasta, the *Calamari Vinaigrette* is tender and lightly dressed.

Among the fish items, *Petrale* in a couple of versions and *Sand Dabs* are highly recommended; the waiters are very good about explaining variations (necessary, since their nomenclature can be whimsical, especially to a non-Italian). *Saltimbocca*, featuring that prosciutto, very good cheese, and another of those marvelous sauces, is also outstanding. Vegetables here vary with the season, but are always slightly undercooked, which is a rare enough virtue.

Desserts are all a cut above the ordinary, especially *Cannoli* and *Semifreddo*, a highly sinful cake.

The wine list is one of the best in North Beach, maybe *the* best, with a great many older selections at reasonable prices. Service is quite good.

North Beach Restaurant is open from 11:30 AM to 11:45 PM every day, and reservations are suggested. Prices are moderate to expensive. Major credit cards are accepted; there is full bar service and valet parking.

622 RISTORANTE ITALIANO

622 Green Street (between Powell and Stockton)
392-3645

The marquee says "since 1934," and from the way old North Beachers tell it, the place has maintained a low profile most of that time—a tradition which continues. It's easy to walk right by the place, unaware that there's a restaurant lurking behind its plain facade.

The general air of anonymity prevails inside, too. You enter through a long, relatively unadorned bar, paneled in dark wood, and from there proceed into a warm and dimly lighted dining room with odd alcoves and spaces around the edges which suggest that someone once did a slapdash renovation or expansion and ended with a haphazard floor plan.

There is an extensive and moderately priced menu, but as it is à la carte, it can mount up. Some of the pastas (made on the premises) are interesting, and this would be a good choice for an inexpensive light meal. Especially notable is *Panzotti*—oversized ravioli, rarely seen any more.

Complete dinners are a bargain, and feature house specials such as *Veal della Casa* and *Chicken Crespano*. The veal is sautéed and drenched in a thickened lemon-butter sauce with bits of prosciutto and pimento, while the chicken is a boned breast stuffed with rice, prosciutto, and mushrooms, napped with rich brown sauce. Both dishes are accompanied by a green vegetable.

But let us begin at the beginning of a complete dinner. Soup, usually minestrone, heavier on vegetables than beans; pasta, *al dente* thank goodness, with a spicy, thin sauce and generous amounts of cheese; a salad of lettuce, with julienned cold cooked carrots and tomato wedges; French bread and real sweet butter; and for dessert, *Frolla alla Crema*, flaky puff pastry filled with almond paste, topped with chocolate, and dusted with powdered sugar. Coffee, inexplicably, is extra.

The wine list is another pleasant surprise: quite a good selection, at quite reasonable prices, with some wines you won't find on other lists (at least the Californians). Service is genial and, in keeping with the general run of things, somewhat confused. In fact, considering everything, it's pleasantly amazing that the place actually works.

622 Ristorante Italiano is open for lunch Tuesday through Saturday from 11:30 AM to 2:30 PM, and for dinner Tuesday through Sunday from 6:00 PM to 11:00 PM, although the bar is open later. Prices are moderate. Reservations are advised, major credit cards accepted, full bar service offered. There is a charge for valet parking.

SWISS LOUIS

Pier 39 (Upper Level)
421-2913

There really is a Swiss Louis, as well as a Swiss John (both Italian-Swiss, of course), and both have a long background in cooking around San Francisco. They came to roost on Broadway over twenty years ago, just a few steps in time before the topless/schlock boom that busted the street.

Swiss Louis (the restaurant) was in those days a raffish sort of trattoria, warm, noisy and bustling, that seemed to exemplify most of the best of North Beach. Bottles and bunches of plastic grapes hung in profusion from the ceiling, which just missed looking like a *pergola* (grape arbor). The lighting was dim, and the place was generally noisy and funky—and fun.

A few years ago, a bad fire in the kitchen partially gutted the restaurant, closing it down. Given the time to think things over, surveying what Broadway had become, they decided to set up shop someplace else—at the brand new development, Pier 39.

The new restaurant is spick-and-span, spacious, with great views of fishing boats and the bay through its wide windows. There are high ceilings with nary a tacky decoration in sight, and the table linens are a spotless white. All these virtues add up to a place with the charm and gusto of a dentist's waiting room. It seems the spirit of North Beach can't be transplanted, at least not to this cold body. Another piece of bad news is that the prices are a trifle high.

On the other hand, the food is still good, and there is the unique and delicious *Mustard Culotte Steak*—a thick whole cut finished at tableside, rapidly sliced and swirled in the escaping meat juices as they blend with the spices: an instant sauce, light but intense. This alone is worth the trip.

Some other specialties preserved from the old days and well worth trying are *Fettuccine alla Matteo*, tossed with peas and bits of ham, coated with a creamy cheese sauce; *Sweetbreads* that are among the best in town, carefully cleaned, lightly sautéed with chopped parsley and mushrooms and not drowned in sauce; and a spicy version of *Saltimbocca*. All meats come with slightly undercooked vegetables, fresh and prepared to order. Clearly, the guiding hands in the new kitchen are talented ones. An old standby dessert is *Strawberries in Port Wine*, and espresso is available.

The wine list is not long, somewhat cryptic, and consists mostly of familiar names, reasonably priced.

Swiss Louis is open for lunch and dinner, from 11:30 AM to 10:00 PM, seven days a week. Prices are moderate to expensive. Major credit cards are accepted, reservations recommended. There is full bar service. There is a parking garage across the street from the main entrance to Pier 39.

TOMMASO'S

1042 Kearny Street (near Broadway)
398-9696

Tomasso's is not only named after a Chinese gentleman, it also serves the best pizza west of the Rockies and could compete nobly anywhere else.

For years it was "Lupo's," owned and run by the genial Frank Cantalupo, and before Broadway became a fen of iniquity it was one of the area's bright stars. Now it upholds honest tradition almost alone. When Cantalupo retired, he sold the place to his Chinese cook, who renamed it more or less after himself and sold it a few years later to an Italian family as dedicated to quality and he and Frank had been.

Because of Tommaso's justifiable popularity, it is best to get here early unless you want to wait; as the foyer is small, waiting frequently involves standing outside.

Wooden booths and large oil paintings line the walls, and long tables fill the middle of the small room, the back of which is dominated by the brick oven that makes the pizzas and calzones so wonderful.

This is not just a pizza parlor, though; a variety of other dishes are offered, which I always swear I'm going to get around to. Among the appetizers to try are *Coo-Coo Clams*. No one remembers how they got the name, but they are baked in white wine with herbs and a little pepper, and they are as good as they are different.

Now, about the pizza: There are as many combinations as can be imagined without stretching tradition, and we leave those combinations to you while we talk about pizza basics. Begin with the brick oven and hot coals of oak; those bricks give back as good as they got over the years. Then the dough—neither the shirt-cardboard crust nor the thick ersatz bread smeared with canned sauce and supermarket mozzarella meant to satisfy those reared on junk food, but a smoky orb, of a thickness just right to carry its burden without ever lapsing into sogginess, and of a satisfying resistance to the tooth. Gilding this lily is a rich and tangy homemade sauce which includes some olive oil, and good assertive cheese that doesn't get ropy or clumped. From this point, you're on your own, but whatever you choose will be fresh and of the best quality.

The *Calzone* here is so rich and dense, inside that same terrific crust, that there should be a law against it. Two kinds of cheese, sausages, tomato sauce spiced with nutmeg . . . Certainly unique, as would be the person who could eat a whole one.

If you can manage dessert, try the homemade *Cannoli*, also unique. It is as rich and dense as everything else here, bursting from a soft crust.

The wine list is good, perhaps too good—who wants Cabernet Sauvignon with pizza and the other simple fare? It is also a little expensive. The house wine is decent and reasonably priced, and a better buy. The service is attentive and friendly.

Tommaso's is open from 5:00 PM to 11:00 PM Wednesday through Saturday, and from 4:00 PM to 10:00 PM on Sunday. It is closed on Monday and Tuesday. Prices are moderate. Major credit cards are accepted, but reservations are not. Beer and wine only.

THE U.S. RESTAURANT

431 Columbus Avenue (at Stockton)
362-6251

There are people who swear by the U.S., and there are people who swear at it; no one is neutral. Suffice it to say that the place has been there for many years and is still going strong.

It can't be because of the decor, which is non-existent, or the service, which is harried and not cheerful, or the ambience, which is a cross between backstage at an Italian opera and a truck-stop cafe. It might be because the prices are low, the portions enormous, and the bleakness of the joint such an irresistible challenge to having a good time.

There are three dining rooms: you step directly into the largest as you enter, and usually go into an elaborate tango with someone trying just as hard to get out. You are told to sit anywhere. Just when you think you'll never be found, up steps a waitress to take your order, frequently before you're ready to give it. She doesn't write anything down, increasing your sense of unease, but the food arrives quickly. If you wish to modify your order in any way, keep your wits about you and speak up right away, before you're abandoned again.

There are nightly specials, which include *Baccala, Osso Buco, Stewed Rabbit, Coteghino*, and other dishes. The earlier you arrive, the better they are likely to be. The rabbit comes in a good spicy sauce, and the osso buco has some authority. If you have a side dish of pasta, you'll enjoy the peppery mushroom/tomato sauce that covers it. There is a wide range of pastas, and there are numerous veal dishes. The pesto sauce is good, heavy and garlicky. There are also a number of short-order dishes.

There is a brief wine list—made up mostly of inexpensive old favorites from California and France—and a fair selection of beers.

The U.S. Restaurant is open from 7:00 AM to 9:00 PM Tuesday through Saturday. Prices are inexpensive. No reservations or credit cards accepted. Beer and wine only.

VANESSI'S

498 Broadway (at Kearny)
421-0890

Vanessi's is a North Beach institution, and has been since Joe Vanessi founded it in 1936. It is popular, usually quite crowded, and not especially welcoming, and it has a very ambitious menu, parts of which are somewhat inaccurate. The very good Chinese-style fried rice which accompanies some dishes, for example, is called "risotto," and "fra diavolo sauce" is emphatically, blandly not.

There are three rooms. You enter by way of the counter room (and the counter is the best place to sit, if you can get a space). There is a room containing the bar and some tables to your left, and there is a quieter dining room at the rear. If you can get a place at the bar the inevitable wait is easier.

Vanessi's wouldn't be an institution without doing something right, and a number of the dishes bear consideration. *Maritata Soup*, for example, a rich cheese broth shot through with delicate strands of pasta; in Italian it is "wedding soup," and it's usually reserved for special occasions.

Several chicken dishes are very good, too—especially the *Chicken Toscana*—and the hamburgers are among the best in town. Try for a seat at the counter and order almost anything sautéed, and you'll be in good shape.

The wine list is outstanding, with quite a good selection of Italian and California wines, most of them at reasonable prices. The service tends to be rather harried, but friendly most of the time.

Vanessi's is open from 11:30 AM to 1:30 AM Monday through Saturday, and from 4:30 PM to midnight on Sunday. Prices range from moderate to expensive. Reservations are strongly advised; major credit cards accepted. Full bar service.

VENETO

Mason and Bay
986-4553

Veneto was founded in 1922, around the time the restaurant boom at
nearby Fisherman's Wharf was underway, and it has operated continu-
ously ever since.

The current owner, Gary Stanton, is firmly on the side of North
Beach tradition, and proves it with his own background: he began at
Veneto as a busboy, worked his way up, took time out to attend hotel
and restaurant school back East, and returned to buy the place. He
wisely retained the chef, Louis Tozzi, who has been there for more
than thirty years.

The restaurant is large, and the mood created is as sentimental as a
tenor aria. A large collection of dolls adorns artfully lighted shelves
and windows. In the Gondola Room, a real gondola floats in its own
canal, murals of Venice (quite realistic) grace all the walls, and opera is
sung every Friday and Saturday night from nine o'clock on. The
lighting is low-key, and dark wood and dark colors prevail. It's quite a
romantic spot at night.

The Gondola Room's roof can be rolled back on good, clear days,
transforming the room into a very Italianate patio.

The best beginning to a meal here is the *antipasto* tray. You get cold,
crisp celery, carrot curls, peppers, black olives, and garbanzo beans—
along with chunks of crabmeat, salami, good prosciutto, slices of
cheese, and radishes—on a bed of lettuce, all dressed with herbs, oil
and vinegar.

While the menu is eclectic, an effort has been made to present many
dishes in the Venetian style. For example, with many you get wild rice
instead of pasta. *Saltimbocca* is presented flat—not rolled as in so many
places in San Francisco—in a thick brown sauce that is the essence of
cooked-down mushrooms.

Chicken Parmigian is not the pedestrian dish it could be; in fact it
probably ought to have another name. It is coated with good cheese,
but the sauce is brown, robust, and only slightly tangy, indicating that
tomatoes aren't the major component. Crisp outside, tender and juicy
inside, it's a good mix of textures and flavors.

Among the desserts, *Fried Cream* and *Spumoni Cake* stand out. The
fried cream is crisp and brown on the outside and moist and tender on

the inside, delivered flambéed; even in small portions it is sinfully rich. The spumoni cake is merely a delightful variation, Italian style, on any ice-cream cake, but is just that much better.

There are specials every day, and they are definitely worth asking about.

Gary Stanton's father was in the wine trade, and that background shows in the list of wines he has chosen. Especially strong on good California selections, it has other well-chosen wines, too. The prices of the wines are quite reasonable.

The service is attentive and friendly. Much of the staff has been here for years.

Veneto is open Tuesday through Sunday, from 11:30 AM to 3:00 PM and from 4:30 to 11:00 PM. Prices are moderate to expensive. Full bar service. Reservations advised, major credit cards accepted. There is valet parking.

WASHINGTON SQUARE
BAR & GRILL

1707 Powell Street (between Union and Columbus)
982-8123

The Washington Square Bar & Grill was established in 1973, but from the beginning it utilized the talents, techniques, and recipes of three long-established North Beach chefs, so the food fits in comfortably with much of the neighborhood tradition.

There are two large, plain rooms—the saloon side, with a long walnut bar, tables, and an enormous mirror over the piano; and the dining room. The ceilings are high, and this helps keep the place comfortable when it's crowded, which it usually is.

From nine o'clock onwards every night, pianists play various styles of jazz, and there are occasional jam sessions and guest artists.

The owners are notable characters. Sam Deitsch is the short, bearded one with the tailored blazer, Levi's, and sneakers, master of the swift and usually cutting retort. Ed Moose is the large, affable, rumpled Irishman with a fondness for suspenders, improbable plaids, and good wine. Mary Etta Moose is responsible for the kitchen, the fresh flowers every day, and a three-octave laugh.

The food tilts heavily toward veal and fish and good pasta. A lot of creative energy goes into the ever-changing daily specials, which also function as a testing ground for new additions to the menu, or merely as someplace to put a great buy at the market that morning. Weekend brunches feature innovative, Italian-oriented egg dishes such as the *North Beach Omelette*, a basil-and-cream-cheese fantasy.

The service is very good if sometimes harried at peak periods, and the wine list is innovative, ever-changing, and reasonably priced.

The Washington Square Bar & Grill is open seven days a week, from 10:30 AM to 2:00 AM. Lunch is served from 11:30 AM to 2:30 PM, and dinner from 6:00 to 11:00 PM. Prices are moderate. Reservations are recommended. Major credit cards are accepted. There is full bar service, and validated parking is available at a garage around the corner, at Filbert and Columbus.

North Beach Coffeehouses

New York has always had a lot of coffeehouses, but in New York you get chess along with your cappuccino, and "coffeehouse" there also means a chess-player or style of playing marked by brilliance, aggression, and eccentricity. Just as that accurately captures the spirit of lower Manhattan, so do the thoroughly Italianate, laid-back *caffes* here capture the more benign spirit and flavor of North Beach.

There are more than a dozen caffes in North Beach, and several are new. (There is something of a Renaissance going on, praise be.) Many serve wine and beer in addition to a range of coffees, chocolates, and teas. All of them serve some food—usually sandwiches and other similar light foods. Some are real neighborhood joints where the casual visitor, especially non-Italian, will not be drawn into the ambience. Most, however, feature the perfect North Beach mix of opposites attracting, elective affinities, and anything goes. Here are seven favorites.

BOHEMIAN CIGAR STORE

566 Columbus Avenue

At the corner of Union Street and Columbus Avenue, the Bohemian combines the atmosphere of a hole-in-the-wall with that of a room with a view (the view being mostly of Washington Square, across the street). The place is fifty years old and looked it until a recent refurbishing, but the regulars will undoubtedly scruff it up pretty well before long. There are a dozen bar stools and half a dozen tables, and there is frequently a lot of banter back and forth, especially when Paolo is behind the bar. Cappuccino is outstanding here, and the pastries are made at home by Liliana, Paolo's mother, and are worth a trip from anywhere—excellent examples of Italian home baking.

CAFFE PUCCINI

411 Columbus Avenue

This is one of the newest caffes brightening up the block between
Vallejo and Green streets, and it is a great spot for people-watching
thanks to its angular layout and large windows. The decor is minimal,
with large ferns hanging above the windows and a few pictures and
decorations on the walls; the effect is of more tidiness than is usual,
but it's still comfortable. A specialty of the house here is sandwiches
on *focaccetta*, a Tuscan-style bread baked in thin, flat loaves, with an
intriguing, slightly sweet taste; prosciutto sandwich is especially
good. There is a pretty good selection of average and not especially
Italian pastry, and an above-average selection of coffees. Try *Espresso
con Panna* and get a strong, small cup of coffee with a lump of cold,
densely rich cream—eat some of the cream and let the rest dissolve.
The jukebox is a marvelous collection of operatic music.

CAFFE ROMA

414 Columbus Avenue

Across the street from Puccini, Caffe Roma is also fairly new,
although the building itself dates back to the rebirth of the city. It was
erected as a bakery after the 1906 fire and earthquake, and was adorned
shortly thereafter with a set of beautiful murals. Time and changing
fortunes worked a number of changes on the building and the block
and the artwork, but a few years ago Sergio Azzolini bought the
building, discovered just what a treasure he had, and restored the
murals while setting up the place. Caffe Roma combines the best
aspects of a coffeehouse with American practicality; where else in
town can you get a good omelette first thing in the morning, and
follow it with a cup of cappuccino, for example. There is a limited
menu, comprised mostly of sandwiches and pizzas. With sandwiches
you get a nice assortment of cold vegetables in an oil-and-vinegar
dressing, a nice touch. There is a very good range of coffees and
especially teas. There are quite a few tables, and as the place is quite
popular, you may have to share one, but that's a fine old North Beach
caffe custom, too.

CAFFE TRIESTE

609 Vallejo

Caffe Trieste is, simply, a tradition. More than twenty years ago, when a whole lot of us were feeling (and sowing) our oats and making bad rhymes in Greenwich Village and other pockets of Bohemianism, the Trieste was an obligatory stop, one of the places where you checked in when you hit town. It wears the patina of age and argument and congeniality and hot air very well, and is just a little quieter now. A large, faded mural dominates the back wall, burnished by time and smoke into something charming. The wall adjacent brings you down to earth in a hurry—a wacky montage of photos of the great, near-great, notorious, and friends. This is a neighborhood place that's accessible, if you can find a seat. Large windows let in a lot of light, and the place is quite cheery despite its plainness. Situated at the corner of Vallejo and Grant, it's a good spot for people-watching, inside and out. Customers tend to the literary much of the time, reading, writing, or talking about reading and writing. Besides the usual range of hot coffees, there is a good selection of iced ones, no less strong and flavorful. The annex next door sells coffee beans and coffee-making accessories.

ENRICO'S

504 Broadway

Enrico Banducci is a North Beach institution on his own, patron saint of entertainers and other artists, fond of good listeners, and a thoroughgoing *bon vivant*. Enrico's is a lot of things: not a bad restaurant, with a rather eclectic menu, some of which is Italian; a fairly good saloon, depending on the crowd, which can tilt heavily toward tourists, due to its Broadway location; and a damn good sidewalk cafe. There is a full range of coffees (though a lot of the emphasis is on coffee/liqueur combinations), and there is a wonderfully odd collection of milkshakes and other such drinks featuring liqueurs. The best choice of all, early in the day or late at night: Enrico's Special, his own variation of a Joe's—enlivened by water chesnuts and tomatoes—with a cappuccino. The hamburgers here are also notable. Enrico is the handsome fellow with the beret.

MALVINA

512 Union

Always called Malvina's, this congenial place is on Union Street, just downhill from Grant. For reasons known only to Franco Bruno, it was recently renovated, but didn't lose any of its charm; the basic aspect of stone, brick, and cheeriness still prevails. There is a good range of coffees and teas here, and the pastries are notable; this is a place to comfortably linger. The staff roasts and grinds coffee for sale to local restaurants, and that expertise is evident in every cup you get in the caffe.

TOSCA CAFE

242 Columbus Avenue

Tosca is an oddity, possesssed of a kind of fierce eccentricity that makes you either chuckle out loud and settle in or flee. A long narrow bar, watched over by two espresso machines of the old-fashioned kind, opens on to a room flanked by booths and furnished with Bauhaus-style tubular furniture which you haven't seen the likes of in years, and which is not at all compatible with the murals on the walls and the dim lighting. The jukebox will undoubtedly be playing an operatic aria, the waitress will be diffident, and the cappuccino will be laced with brandy unless you specify otherwise. (There is a full bar.) I usually specify cappuccino with anisette, and settle in.

The Food Shops
of North Beach

by Mary Etta Moose

The Butchers, the Bakers,
the Parmesan Graters

BIORDI ART IMPORTS

CAVALLI BOOKSHOP

GOURMET GUIDES BOOKSHOP

CUNEO BAKERY

DANILO BAKERY

ITALIAN FRENCH BAKERY

LIGURIA BAKERY

STELLA PASTRY

VICTORIA BAKERY

R. IACOPI BUTCHER

ITALIAN VILLAGE MARKET

LITTLE CITY MARKET

WASHINGTON SQUARE MEAT MARKET

GRAFFEO COFFEE COMPANY

The Delicatessens of North Beach

FLORENCE RAVIOLI FACTORY

GLORIA SAUSAGE FACTORY & DELICATESSEN

ITALIAN VILLAGE DELICATESSEN

MOLINARI

PANELLI BROTHERS DELICATESSEN

ROSSI'S MARKET

The Butchers, the Bakers, the Parmesan Graters

An Introduction to Shops Carrying Foods and Related Items

There's a selection of shops in North Beach in every category of culinary want—and one goes to a different shopkeeper for almost everything: a certain bakery for a certain bread, another for a favorite kind of biscotti, yet another for the best breadstick. One can easily visit four delicatessens in shopping for the go-withs for a single meal, on the way to more than one butcher's for assembling the entrée course.

Figone Hardware can be counted on for certain old-time Italian kitchen gadgets that one would not expect Biordi—let alone Columbus Cutlery—to carry.

The North Beach shopper does not have the supermarket mentality. And prices in these neighborhood shops are much lower than the same specialty items cost in gourmet shops in other parts of town.

BIORDI ART IMPORTS

412 Columbus Avenue, between Stockton and Vallejo
392-8096
HOURS: Mon–Sat, 9–6

This little shop has been local headquarters for Italian cookery utensils and machines since 1946. Mr. Biordi first introduced the Etruscan clay pots from Florence in 1965, and current proprietor Giovanni Savio is still the first, and often the only, culinary-utensil buyer in town to bring in unusual Tuscan tools—such as the veal scaloppine press designed to slide off the mucilaginous European-style white veal without mutilating it.

You'll find every size and type of pasta machine, as well as ravioli plates and markers, a cavatelli maker, pastry and pasta form cutters and rollers, a tool for forming homemade cialde, cheese graters (not only graters, but the types of graters indigenous to various regions of Italy), espresso makers, the Carrara marble *mortaio e pestello* (mortar and pestle) that Italian home cooks still use to macerate their basil for pesto (God forbid the herb should touch metal!), coffee and pepper grinders, a wine press, a zucchini corer, a tomato press, pizza cutters, garlic presses, meat grinders, poppy-seed grinders for pastry, cannoli tubes, bottle corkers, pasta tongs and strainers, ad infinitum.

There's an extensive collection of Majolica ware, the colorful provincial ceramic and porcelain tableware with serving dishes of all shapes and sizes. A few of the hard-to-find beauties from Italy's great porcelain maker, Ginori, are here, and Mr. Savio will order for you from Ginori's catalogues. From Venice are Murano crystal wine and liqueur glasses, chandeliers and mirrors, as well as hundreds of small gift items. Everything can be shipped throughout the U.S.

CAVALLI

1441 Stockton
421-4219
HOURS: Mon–Sat, 9–5:45

While you're walking through North Beach, peek into Cavalli's window. The owners bring in cookbooks from Italy, some in Italian, some in English, most of them books you'll not see elsewhere around town. They are frequently marked down in price.

GOURMET GUIDES

1767 Stockton, at Greenwich
391-5903
HOURS: Mon–Fri, 12–5; Sat, 12–3

It is relevant to mention here Jean Bullock's cookbook store, a most welcome addition to North Beach. She has a comprehensive collection of books about food and cooking, and responds to orders for a single copy of some obscure book so fast it's baffling. What she ain't got, she can get. Her coverage of Italian cooking is the most thorough I've encountered in San Francisco.

CUNEO BAKERY/ MALVINA CIALDE

523 Green Street
392-4969
HOURS: Daily, 7 AM–6 PM

Renato and Maria Groppi have been at this stand for twenty-five years, making the best hand-rolled extra-long breadsticks in town, as well as the standard-sized sourdough breadsticks they package under the Malvina label (which are the best packaged ones). Maria says they have the only machine in the U.S. for mass-producing cialde, the crisp, hollow-tube-shaped wafers made of slightly sweet egg-butter-and-flour dough, to nibble with caffe latte, or to use as spoons to scoop up zabaglione, or to fill with ice cream (they were the original ice cream cone) or with whipped cream flavored with crushed fruit. Baked daily are both sweet and sour French bread and rolls, seeded bread and Italian egg bread and focaccia. On Wednesdays and Saturdays they add whole-wheat bread to their production, and on Fridays they make Italian corn-flour bread. There's panettone and buccellato and, at Easter, three special breads: Cicciotti, Colomba di Pasquale; and a Tuscan specialty called Pasimata, a wavy screw-shaped bread made with butter, eggs, and anise seed. They make Galetti, the sourdough hardtack used by Italians for soups, chowders, and croutons; breakfast pastries; several flavors of glazed fruit tortas; assorted cookies, including a giant macaroon; and Italian pastries, including a chocolate-and-spice-filled spiral. Here you'll find the two dusky Tuscan tortas: the Lucca Torta di Verdura, and the Florentine Torta di Riso (see **Glossary**). They also stock some of the Della Santina pasta line, and the Alita brand domestic pastas. Take out only.

DANILO BAKERY

516 Green Street, between Columbus and Grant, at Bannon Alley
989-1906
HOURS: Mon–Sat, 7–6, Sundays, 7–5

Established in 1907, this shop has flourished under the painstaking proprietorship of Danilo Di Piramo from Tuscany for more than a dozen years. Danilo turns out a remarkable array of breads, and then makes *biscotti di pane* (rusks) from every one of them. Here you can assemble a diverting sampler of breads for a bread, cheese, and wine party. The breads are made in many shapes and sizes, including the classic Italian sesame twist, and a novelty shape like a five-fingered hand, for a maximum of crusty portions. The doughs are a regular French (not sourdough) and a sweet French (with a little sugar and oil added to the bread dough), called pane olio. Italian-style corn-flour bread and whole-wheat bread are made on Saturdays only. There are three versions of panettone: plain, with anise or raisin, as well as Pan Dolce Genovese, a panettone made with anise, glazed fruit, and raisins. Anise-flavored Buccellato, an egg bread with citron, is made both in a ring shape and in a small oval loaf. Danilo's salty, crisp breadsticks are all handmade, using a special grissini dough, rather than bread dough. At Easter they feature Cicciotti, the egg bread shaped into a little man with an Easter egg in his belly. In addition to the thickly sliced biscotti made from all the above breads, they do the Italian version of melba toast, from a special sweetened anise biscotti dough, and frizelle, a non-sourdough hardtack bread ring, horizontally sliced into two pieces and tied back together. This is sought out by Italians for dipping into soups, bagna cauda, and sauces. Danilo also makes Italian cookies and his two native specialties, the Torta di Verdura and the Torta di Riso. Take out only.

ITALIAN FRENCH BAKERY

1501–1503 Grant, at Union
421-3796
HOURS: Mon–Sat, 8–5; Sundays, 8–12

Francesco Taddeucci bakes every day. He makes the traditional French baguettes—sourdough or sweet—with the proper crusty outside texture, an authentic, consistent French bread. There are also bread rolls and larger loaves. Finely ground fresh French breadcrumbs are made here daily and are available by weight.

On the Italian side are panettone, buccellato, biscotti, and cookies.

LIGURIA BAKERY, SOROCCO & CO.

Corner of Stockton and Filbert, opposite Mama's
421-3786
HOURS: Mon–Sat, 6–6; Sundays, 6–noon. Closed for vacation
during the last two weeks of August.

Liguria Sorocco was established right after the Great Earthquake and
Fire, by Ambrogio Sorocco, and is run now by his son George, with
partners Gene di Matei, Atilio Aste, and Gus Accalini. They bake
focaccia bread all day long, from five in the morning until six at night.
Their enormous red-brick hearth ovens turn out flat sheets of the
inch-thick pizza bread, which is made of flour, water and fresh yeast,
and is brushed with olive oil and coarse salt and baked. It comes plain,
or with raisins, or with a topping of spring onions and tomato sauce.
Because the line of patrons is constant from six AM to closing time,
and the bread is baked in fresh batches all day long, it is always warm
from the oven and tender.

This addicting bread is best eaten as is, but also adapts well to many
uses. It's a tasty base for hearty open-faced sandwiches. A good
change-of-pace breakfast or luncheon entrée that finicky kids will eat is
a bread pudding made from any of the flavors of focaccia, with eggs,
milk, butter, rings of sweet peppers and onions, cheese, and maybe
cooked meat or fish. The World's Best Cheese Sandwich is realized
when plain focaccia, brushed with oil and salt, is baked in a small pie
tin, split hot from the oven and stuffed with a slab of full-ripe teleme
cheese, wrapped and set aside a few minutes, and promptly served in
salty, oozing wedges. (See the **Recipe Section** for the complete
recipe.) Many a Washington Square picnic and working lunch comes
from the Sorocco, with wine or a beverage from the Napoli Market a
few doors down on Stockton. Focaccia graces parties and weddings, as
well. Take out only.

STELLA PASTRY

446 Columbus, between Green and Vallejo
986-2914
HOURS: Mon, 7–6; Tues–Sat, 8–6; Sundays, 8–2

Stella has ornamented North Beach for thirty-five years, and the tire-lessly innovative Franco Santucci has presided for twenty of them, since his arrival from Lucca. His airy creations boast a light hand with sugar, and liqueurs are used so subtly they puzzle the palate: one cannot be quite certain what has contributed the delicate flavors. His best-known specialty is the Sacripantina, a dome-shaped white cloud made of many layers of thin strips of *genoise* (Italian spongecake) and a cold zabaglione made with Marsala, rum and maraschino liqueur, the whole masked with whipped cream. It also comes in individual portion cups (either your own or his), or, with twenty-four hours' notice, in sizes to serve from four to twenty-five. Franco learned to make it at the Preti Bakery in Genoa, which was its creator, and is now closed. It is available nowhere else. His gallery of wedding cakes includes a tiered St. Honore, and twenty-four hours' notice can produce a memorable Zuppa Inglese or Croquembouche. Pastries include cannoli, raspberry or pineapple puffs, ovale custard puffs, cheesecake, almond tortas, gesuits, French croissants, and an elaborate array of Italian cookies.

Two of Franco's latest creations are the "Torronino" and the "Delicia Stella." Torronino is individual portions of a nougat-flavored cream combined with cold zabaglione and crushed torrone—the Italian nougat candy—on a genoise base.

Though cheese is an ingredient of the Delicia Stella, it is not to be confused with cheesecake as we know it. A *pasta frolla crostata* (Italian pie crust) contains a layer of genoise, upon which is heaped an unbaked, flavored, and whipped concoction of cheese and cream, at once so light and so dense it's like a new texture. The Delicia comes *multi-saffrita* (in several flavors): chocolate mousse, strawberry, or pineapple, with a fourth flavor in the works. The fruit-flavored versions are topped with the corresponding fruits.

At Christmastime, the panettone are baked in tall molds and topped with *pignoli*, European style—and at Easter there are several sizes of

Colomba di Pasquale. You'll find boxed and bulk Italian candies, selections of *bomboniere* (favors) for every special occasion, "confetti" gold and silver Jordan almonds for anniversaries, and finnocchiette candies for boys' baptisms. Call ahead for special cakes, and put your order in early for all holiday breads and pastries. Stella has hot coffee, one table and two chairs.

VICTORIA BAKERY

1362 Stockton, at Vallejo
781-2015
HOURS: Daily, 8–6
Delivery service available

Showers, christenings, first communions, graduations, weddings, anniversaries, retirements—Victoria has been sweetening every occasion in its customers' lives since 1910. Great-grandchildren of original customers still place their wedding-cake orders to take to their current abodes, as far away as Sacramento. Owner Renzo Lavezzo—who learned his baking in Chiavari, Genoa—took over in 1947. The most popular items here are the rum cake, the St. Honore, a fedora cake, and special occasion creations. There are Italian cookies, macaroon tortas, many Italian pastries, cannoli, and sweet Italian croissants, most of which are served in many of our local coffeehouses. Renzo always bakes panettone, and, at Easter, Colomba di Pasquale. Twenty-four hours' notice is required for Zuppa Inglese. There is always a freezerful of zuccotto, a dome-shaped concoction of liqueur-soaked fruit and filbert-studded genoise, layered with buttercream. Boxed, imported candies and a large array of tiny toys for favors, gift wrapping, and decorations are also available. Take out only.

R. IACOPI & SON

1460 Union, at Grant
421-0757
HOURS: Daily, 10–6, except Wed & Sun

My introduction to North Beach cooking came twenty years ago from
Bruno Iacopi, who for fifteen cents sold me a slab of lamb ribs, tossed
in a branch of fresh rosemary and a head of green garlic, and said,
"Now, all you need is the olive oil and wine." Since 1911, many a
young cook has garnered direction from the generous Iacopi expertise.
Bruno was born in North Beach in 1915 to Rudolpho and Nella
Iacopi. He joined Rudolpho in the shop in 1937, for a stay interrupted
only by an Army stint during World War II.

This is an individualistsic, custom butcher shop. No meat is pre-
cut. Even hamburger meat is chosen by the customer and ground
before him. The twenty-foot ceiling is ringed with a bar from which
hang enormous branches of fresh rosemary, house-cured Parma hams
(prosciutto), and house-made sausages: Toscana (with garlic), Sicilian
(with anise), and Calabrese (hot). The walls are painted with a mural
of a pasture overlooking Rudolpho's native Gattaiola, Lucca. (He had
the town's church wired for electricity before he died in 1971.)

Bruno's beef is prime, and well aged. On display are fabricated cuts:
whole thirty-pound short-loin beef porterhouse and whole prime ribs,
to be cut into steaks or roasts; calf and beef livers; raw and smoked
lamb; calf and beef tongues; raw and smoked pork loins and hams;
and the picnic hams and prosciutto Bruno himself cures from fresh
hams and then treats in a solution to leach out extra salt, leaving a
creamy, sweet ham.

He was known as "The Capretto King of North Beach" in the old
days when he sent scouts into the Sonoma hills to hand-select his baby
goats, and, in these less-Italian times, he still stocks capretto in season,
from a jobber. He offers this hint for barbecuing a kid: "Just before
done, baste with olive oil and wine vinegar to which lemon juice and
minced garlic and rosemary are added."

He'll suggest you try baking his sausages in red wine, or add them
to your next barbecue, or cook them with eggplant, garlic, tomato,
and red wine for a pasta sauce, or, for a spicy change, add them to
your own meatloaf recipes or to your meatballs (and then stuff your

sautéed tiny meatballs into some cooked jumbo pasta shells, before saucing, for an attractive presentation).

LAMB SHANK FANS! In these days when it's impossible to find meaty lamb shanks, you'll be glad to know that Bruno will cut them for you with the meaty round-bone still attached at the top. He will, in fact, cut you any cut you know how to ask for. He even puts out the Butcher's Steak, for any customer who knows one when he sees it. So named because there's only one to a cow and the butcher always takes it home, the Butcher's Steak is a small (16 to 20 oz.) muscle from the left hindquarter. It's very tender, for pan grilling. It makes a fine steak tartare, and its sweetish taste would win you first prize in a chili cookout.

His Petaluma eggs come brown or white, and seem always to be double-yolked. The flavorful chickens are Petaluma birds. There are no identifying markers or price tags here, but deals are fair.

ITALIAN VILLAGE MARKET

490 Columbus, at Green
421-1798
HOURS: Mon–Sat, 8–7; Sundays, 9–6

This old North Beach institution is, for the nonce, under absentee ownership, but its resident personalities Bobby Silvestre and his buddy, Carlos, are keeping the produce section stocked the way a good Italian grocer should, and Art Barni's butcher concession obliges the Italian trade by fleshing out his meat collection with fresh fish and a reliable stock of the hard-to-gets: calf brains, sweetbreads, tongue, variety meats, oxtails, rabbits, and squab. The delicatessen is also in good, hardworking hands, as reported in that section of this book.

LITTLE CITY MARKET

1400 Stockton, at Vallejo
986–2601 or 397–6854
HOURS: Mon–Sat, 10–5

"Ron the Butcher" Spinali (of KCBS Radio fame) and his staff pride themselves on their professional, one-to-one attention to each customer. As the window-card recipes signal before you enter the shop, they're quick to respond to your questions about meat cookery. Ron has mimeographed copies of his original recipes on hand to give out, and adds one new recipe to his collection each year. He carries Eastern pork, and specializes in Eastern-style meat-cutting, which, he reports, brings him a clientele of relocated Easterners from all over the Bay Area.

This is the North Beach source for "rose" veal (see VITELLO in the **Glossary**). Ron stocks a "filet roast" of veal, and keeps the whole "filets" on prominent display. This tender veal cut makes excellent scaloppine. See the **Recipe Section** for a scaloppine that will be new to you.

WASHINGTON SQUARE MEAT MARKET

659 Union, between Columbus and Powell
362-0466
HOURS: Mon–Sat, 10–6

An excellent Toscana-style (with garlic) Italian sausage is made by proprietor Ping Leong, at this shop opposite Washington Square Park. This is also North Beach's source for Provimi brand European-style milk-fed veal. The display case always has fish in season, rabbits, and Petaluma chickens and eggs.

GRAFFEO COFFEE COMPANY

733 Columbus, between Greenwich and Filbert
986-2420
HOURS: Mon–Fri, 9–6; Sat, 9–5

Proprietor Luciano Repetto's father Giovanni bought this unique coffee emporium, established in 1935, after John Graffeo's death in 1943. The formula for the Graffeo blend was selected by Giovanni's father ninety-five years ago. Repetto worked the ships in the days before coffee came in cans, when sailors picked up raw coffee beans whenever they were in a port and roasted them aboard ship. Repetto experimented with combinations of coffees for years until he came up with the five kinds still used in this shop's superb blend: Costa Rican, Colombian, and Nicaraguan (Madagalpa District), and coffees from Papua, New Guinea and Java. Proclaims Giovanni: "The chemicals are the same in all beans, $C^8H^{10}N^4O^2$. But all beans are not the same."

When Luciano Repetto took over from his father, he was dissatisfied with the then-prevalent methods of roasting (with flame and timers) and the sometimes scorched and bitter flavors they can impart to coffee. He knew there had to be some new coffee technology developing out there somewhere, and he researched the chemical engineering trade journals, where he discovered that one of the world's foremost authorities on coffee (and now a Graffeo customer), Mike Sivetz, was up in Oregon experimenting with a new method. So he hopped on a plane, roasted coffee in Mike's garage, and came home the same weekend with the new machine. One of seven in the United States, it uses hot air rather than flame, and, instead of being operated by a timer, has a probe which senses temperature and ends the cycle the instant the beans are ready.

Graffeo's makes a remarkably good decaffeinated coffee bean. Their Colombian beans are shipped to Switzerland for removal of caffeine by a new steam process. No chemicals are used, so your pancreas is safe from the chlorinated hydrocarbons the scientists are now warning us about. Then, Luciano roasts the beans in his magic machine, and they produce a pleasant, well-flavored brew.

This little shop ships regular coffee orders to customers (some for twenty-five years now) all over the U.S.A. His roster of clients includes many household words, but Dr. Luciano never reveals the names of his patients.

The Delicatessens
of North Beach

The Italian art of packaging prevails in the visual anarchy of these colorful emporiums. Salamis and Parma hams cascade from twenty-foot ceilings like yummy stalactites in a gourmand's treasure cave. Walls are lined, from floor to ceiling, with brightly garbed canned and dried comestibles from various regions of Italy. Cases of myriad forms of pastas are stacked up in the aisles, opposite the long cold-meat and cheese counters. There are handsome tins of cooking oils, cookies and breads, extensive arrays of Italian wines and aperitivos, jars of dried herbs, and boxes of dried fish and peppers. Compare the prices of specialty "gourmet" items, in downtown and chic shops elsewhere, with North Beach pricetags, and you'll quickly realize that these shop-keepers are not greedy. Bargains are here.

Almost to a man, the clerks are cooks, and generous with recipe ideas and explanations of unfamiliar products. They are quick to offer tasting samples to aid your decisions. They're pleased to see you take an interest in the cuisine, and the time to shop in North Beach.

These festive environments are a visual spur to the appetite. They speak of holidays and feasts, the pleasures of the complex culinary inheritance of northern Italy, and its northern California expression.

FLORENCE RAVIOLI FACTORY

1412 Stockton, between Vallejo and Columbus
421-6170
HOURS: Mon–Sat, 10–6

Florence Ravioli was established after the Earthquake, around 1915, by the Bornaccorsi family from Florence, who sold to John Minetto, from Lucca, thirty-three years ago. Co-owner Louis Martinelli joined Minetto twenty-six years ago.

Pastas here contain eggs and semolina and spinach. The egg and spinach colors are not intensified artificially. The tortellini come fresh or frozen. Fresh daily are ravioli in two sizes, plain and spinach tagliarini, tagliatelle, and fettuccine. They'll cut their dough into any width for you, and will cut it into cannelloni squares if you call ahead. Potato gnocchi are sold frozen only, because they are too tender to handle if unfrozen. Restaurants are the biggest buyers of their fresh pasta; every day commences with a long parade of restaurateurs, picking up their standing orders.

Florence's cheeses are held in a 60°–62° cheese refrigerator and never allowed to take a deeper chill. They have the hard-to-find Cacciocavallo grating cheese, aged four years. They carry Columbus and Gallo sausages and cold meats, and Hormel prosciutto. Minetto cautions that he holds his meats at too cold a temperature for immediate consumption. They should always be given time to come to room temperature, for fullest flavor. He reminds us how good a flavoring agent some of these sausages can be in cooking—for example, mortadella and salami ground up into one's stuffings for meat, pasta, or vegetables, or ground-meat mixtures.

Florence imports a very good line of Italian pasta—Della Santina/Freidani—in myriad, continually changing varieties, in addition to De Cecco, and a full line of the best of the made-in-U.S.A. pastas, our own Alita of Oakland. These are full semolina and egg pastas that hold their own with the best of Italy's.

The entrance corner of the shop is crammed with huge gunnysacks containing a dozen kinds of Italian dried beans, including lupini, cannellini, and fava or horse beans, and dried chestnuts, and squash seeds, to use like pumpkin or sunflower seeds. They carry four varieties of dried mushrooms: California field mushrooms, the South American boletus, the Italian porcini and huge Italian field mushrooms. There are several brands of the pot-bellied rice grown in the Piemonte region of Italy, and an assortment of flours includes chestnut, potato, rice, semolo, and corn.

The world's best biscuits are here: wafers and crackers from all of Europe, grissini, biscotti, cannoli shells, cialde. Canned goods include every kind of canned bean, Progresso's and Homesteads' sauces, soups, and Progresso's fine pear-tomato products. There is also a profusion of Italian candies—hard drops, chews, bar and baking chocolate, gianduiotto (hazelnut wafers), baci (hazelnut kisses), chocolate cordials, torrone, a fruit-and-nut chocolate torta, panforte, cioccorelli (chocolate almond ovals), colombine (chocolate doves), a chocolate-nut spread for bread, marrons glacés, and a marzipan dough ready to be colored and hand-molded into your own fantasies.

GLORIA SAUSAGE FACTORY AND DELICATESSEN

635 Vallejo, between Columbus and Stockton
421-5283
HOURS: Mon–Sat, 9–6

Founded sixty years ago by Frank Maggiora, from Piemonte (the northwest tip of Italy), Gloria is now run by his daughter Alda and her cousin, Cy Miravalle.

The small factory is part of the premises, and Cy still produces Maggiora's recipes for coteghino boiling sausages, salamis, salamettis, sweet fennel sausages, garlic sausage, hot Calabrese sausage, peperoni (a dried Calabrese), a mild French-style white-wine sausage, a French-style Boudin (blood pudding), and a mild Italian-style breakfast-link pork sausage. Alda suggests using the breakfast links in a *Fritto Misto* (mixed fry) platter, with sweetbreads, chicken livers, carrots, and fried cream, with salsa verde. Their display of a wide variety of Italian-and French-style veal, pork, and beef cold cuts includes prosciutto, galantinas, lingua (a tongue loaf), mortadella, zampone, coppa, *mortadella di fegato* (a liver mortadella which comes both coarse-cut and fine-cut with pistachios); a mild pastrami made from beef eye of round; turkey, rare roast beef, and their popular fruited baked ham. They make a fine truffled liver pâté and an unusual frittata, tall and so smooth and meaty it's like a pâté. Their many salad preparations include Gardiniere Tonnato (see the **Recipe Section**), roasted red and yellow sweet peppers, macaroni and vegetable salad, pickled pigs' feet, bean salads, marinated olives of all kinds, and marinated mushrooms and artichokes.

They carry some seventy-five imported cheeses (some hard to find in fancy cheese chops): table (semi-soft) Pecorino; the world's finest

Parmesan cheese, Reggiano Parmigiano—made only during certain months when grass is the sweetest, with milk from special cows, and aged five years; creamy St. André; Torta San Gaudenzio; Gorgonzolas; imported Bel Paese; Fontina d'Aosta; a dry Riccota Pecorino table cheese, and a low-fat, low-salt cheese of surprisingly good flavor.

Sandwiches are made from any combination of meats and cheeses. Gloria makes fresh cheese and beef ravioli daily, and their bottled "gravy" is a meat-and-porcini-mushrooms Ragu Bolognese. The counter shelves titillate with holiday viands—Cremona Mustard Fruits, preserved orange slices, currant and lingonberries, Bar le Duc, white and black truffles, pine nuts, gooseberries, tomato paste in tubes, scungilli, caponata, pickled miniature asparagus spears and eggplants, and relishes. There's a profusion of Italian and French candies, cookies, and herbal teas, and Italian wines and aperitivos. They are closed one week of the year, usually in August. Take out only.

ITALIAN VILLAGE DELICATESSEN

490 Columbus, at Green
421-1798
HOURS: Mon–Sat, 8–7; Sun, 9–6

This concession in Italian Village Market was taken over by Andrew St. Gallen two years ago, when homesickness for North Beach prompted him to sell his popular fifteen-year-old Temescal Delicatessen in Berkeley. He brings in many brands and items not carried elsewhere in the area.

Cheeses include English, French, and Italian—double Gloucesters, cheddars, Stilton, Pont L'Eveque, Scamorze (the hard-to-find, smoky, woodsy ball of cheese, mozzarella-like with a difference). There's an imported panettone with chocolate, Saag's fine line of sausages, chicken on the rotisserie, mixed salads, sandwiches hot and cold, biscuits, and sweets. Homestead's thin-skinned ravioli are here—both the beef and the excellent ones stuffed with a blend of four cheeses and sweet basil.

Andy's a natural, experimental Italian cook, and is full of recipe ideas. He puts lots of effort into keeping an unusually wide selection of Italian wines and aperitivos.

MOLINARI

373 Columbus, at Vallejo
421-2337
HOURS: Mon–Sat, 8–5

Originally established in 1896, this is the most prominently located
and most widely known of the neighborhood's delicatessens. Current
owner Bob Mastrelli is a newcomer by North Beach standards, having
acquired the business in 1963. Most of the cold meats here come from
the Molinari wholesale sausage factory, with some from Columbus,
and with prosciutto hams from Hormel and Citerrio. The usual
cheeses and mixed salads are all here, and the sandwich counter does a
brisk business from opening bell to closing. Green and white tagliarini
and linguine are made fresh daily, as are ravioli and tortellini.
Molinari carries some California and Italian wines; canned and frozen
goods; and Fernet Branca and Brioschi, should anyone overindulge.
Take out only.

PANELLI BROTHERS
DELICATESSEN

1419 Stockton, between Columbus and Vallejo
421-2541
HOURS: Mon–Sat, 9–6

Ernesto and Igilio Panelli established this shop when they arrived from
Lucca in 1934. Their sons Vince, Richard, and Robert grew up
working behind these counters, and took over from their father and
uncle in 1950. Lifelong customers enjoy the old-world continuity of
this family business. The only changes here are in the clientele, once
100 percent Italian, and now 60 percent Chinese and 40 percent
Italian, many of whom are children of original customers. Nothing is
manufactured here, but the brothers Panelli search the market to glean
the best cold meats (mostly from Columbus and Gallo) and cheeses,
treat them with respect and slice them thinly enough. Their volume is
so great that freshness is assured—once cut, a slab of meat or cheese is
never there long enough to lose moisture. Even a prosciutto ham
opened in the morning is gone by evening. Their sandwiches are a
great bargain: four inches thick with meats and cheese, and at a price
that is better than reasonable. They stock salami, salamicotto, coppa,
mortadella, galantina, soppressata (headcheese), zampone (pork- and

beef-stuffed pig's foot), pancetta (rolled, unsmoked bacon, pepper-cured), coteghino, cooked pepper coppa, pastrami, two kinds of birolda (blood-pudding sausage)—the Genovese (to broil, fry or boil) and Toscano (ready to eat, made with raisins and pinenuts), and many more. They carry Hormel (best of the two) and Citerrio prosciuttos, and soak them in a solution to leach out excess salt. They sell 20 of these a week, and sell the bones and fat for Minestrone.

A private butcher makes their three Italian pork sausages without nitrites or preservatives. They grate their own cheeses on the premises, fresh daily, a blend of domestic Parmesan and Romano. Unusual cheeses in their collection are Asiago (a semi-hard table cheese of exceptional flavor) and Locatelli-brand Romano, a sharp but not salty sheeps'milk grating cheese—hurrah for American cheesemakers on both counts.

Panelli is the exclusive retailer for Panama Ravioli Factory's fresh-daily pasta and ravioli, and carries eight brands of imported dried pasta, as well as the excellent Alita, made in the Bay Area. Other unusual finds here are real citron, big jarsful of bulk spice seeds, and three kinds of dried mushrooms: the California field mushroom, the Italian *porcini*, and, the best buy, an intensely flavored South American wild boletus, at one-sixth the price of its relatives. The South American is very dark brown, because, to meet U.S. Department of Agriculture requirements for import, they must be dried first, then brine-soaked and dried again. They should be put into boiling water, cooked two minutes, and drained. (Save the water for cooking, but watch its saltiness.) Mince them very fine, to look more like *duxelles* in your sauce, and to lessen their dark appearance. They take dried mushrooms out of the luxury class and put them back into the sauce-pots of workaday folks. All foods here are for take out only.

ROSSI'S MARKET

627 Vallejo, at Columbus
986–1068
HOURS: Mon–Sat, 8–6
DELIVERIES: Daily except Tuesday

Nate and George Lackman have run this fine Italian market for twenty-five years now. They carry all the staples, spirits, and imported goods the local cuisine demands, and are reliable sources for many unusual items considered basic necessities for holiday cooking in these parts—all at reasonable prices.

The star of their operation is Italo Lucchesi, who gently insinuates the good life of Lucca into all of his endeavors—in this case, the produce department. Italo combs the markets for all the fresh herbs and uncommon produce these northern Italians expect of him, and what's not in the markets, he culls from his own and neighboring gardens. His line-up of produce is an irresistible suggestion to bring to your table the dish of the moment: he'll arrange, side by side, ingredients for a spring vegetable stew of onion, artichoke and two kinds of fresh beans in pods; with the fat green spring onions alongside the baby artichokes (he lays the fresh bay leaves on top of the bin of artichokes so you won't forget to add fresh bay with the lemon juice and flour when you boil them); and fresh fava beans, and shell beans, the fresh cranberry beans that are such fun to open—every pod contains a different pastel color of bean: white, pink, green, lavender, speckled. Or he'll assemble bins of ingredients for a summer salad, with sweet white zucchini, tender yong white asparagus, fresh fave to add raw, radicetta (a flat-leafed endive), cherry tomatoes, and sweet basil for the vinaigrette. You may find wild rapini (boiling greens; use root and all), baby eggplants, oversize figs (both white and black), zucchini flowers (to dip in beaten egg and flour batter and deep-fry a couple of seconds, or to stuff with veal farcé and braise), two-inch zucchinis with a big flower on the end of them, or a zucchini plant in a tin can so you can go home and raise your own flowers.

Italo offers this hint to gardeners: put seeds out by the moon (seven days after it's full, you have twenty-eight days to put them out). Then cover the ground with potato sacks and keep them just damp, and, in this warm womb, radicetta, for instance, will be up in five days.

Italo's pride in "getting nice things, and keeping them right" has enhanced North Beach since he was twelve years old, when he joined his parents, Evo and Pia, at the old Lucchesi Market on Columbus, where we all got our year's supply of braided green garlic, and fresh white truffles, and marinated fresh porcinis. Ah! those were the days.

It may be appropriate to pay tribute here also to the Lucchesi fifteen-year reign at Buon Gusto/Italian Village Delicatessen, where Pia labored in the basement to make such fondly remembered treats as her famous baccala fritters and artichoke frittatas (her recipes for both are included in the **Recipe Section**), polpette, stuffed vegetables, raviolis made with thin skins and the brains and marrow in them, and the traditional Lucca tortas at Christmastime. These are the rich, sound Florentine traditions of the table, transported to, and flourishing still, in our fortunate North Beach.

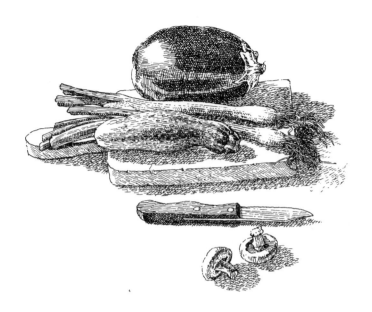

Some North Beach Recipes

by Mary Etta Moose

Cooking lore is only as finite as the number of good cooks. An able cook is always discovering more. In this little Italian corner of the world, people who care about the subject have developed some genuine contributions to the literature.

Cookbook collectors will have many versions of some of these dishes, but comparison will reveal telling differences. Some are the practical developments of professional cooks—others, flights of fancy that settled down to work. The best of our *capi di cucina* (Italian chefs) have an attribute in common: an honesty of preparation that produces consistent dishes with integrity, classics of simplicity that honor each ingredient in the balance they achieve.

My guideline in selecting these recipes and cookery suggestions was not to supply a manual of a local style, but to single out information, variations, and procedures most likely to be new to fellow cooks, and which will reliably produce tasty results. We hope they'll not only be read, but put to use.

A Note About Salt:
Where I consider salt essential to a dish, I specify. Otherwise, drive the salt cellar at your own speed.

A Note About Stocks:
If you must substitute canned broth for chicken or veal stocks, try Swanson's chicken broth. It has a clear flavor and is less salty than its condensed cousin from Campbell's.

A Note About Vinegars:
I frequently specify pear vinegar, which is brewed from pears, and is the softest of all vinegars. It's available by mail order from Harry & David, Medford, Oregon, 97501, and is worth the trouble and expense. An acceptable substitute would be rice wine (sake) vinegar.

A Note About Parmesan Cheese:
The best possible Parmesan taste comes from Reggiano Parmigiano brand from Italy. The best of the domestically made Parmesans is Stella brand Black Wax Parmesan, which is easier on the food budget, when that is the first consideration.

LIST OF RECIPES:

ANTIPASTI:

Gardiniere allo Tonnato
North Beach Fishermen's Salad

BASIL:

Pesto Base
Pasta al Pesto
Quadratti di Basilico
Sweet Basil Vinegar
Conchigliette e Lenticche al Pesto
Sweet Basil Butter
Sweet Basil Cheese Fantasy

SOUP:

Chef Aldo Persich's Minestrone

PASTA, POTATO, AND RICE:

Rissoto di Puntette
Fettuccine Chef Bardelli
Chef Stelvio Storache's Potato Gnocchi
Chef Aldo's Wild Rice

EGGS:

Artichoke Frittata
Vegetarian Joe's Special
North Beach Omelette

FISH:

Italo Lucchesi's Baccala Fritters
Chef Manuel Sausedo's Crab Cioppino and Polenta

BEEF:

Culotte Steak

CHICKEN:

Chef Silvio Conciatore's Chicken Jerusalem
Chef Tulio Rosati's Filetti di Pollo alla Fontina
Chef Tony Penado's Borsa di Pollo Piemontese

PORK:

Sam Deitsch's Fennel-Roasted Pork with Sauerkraut and Red Cabbage

VEAL:

An Autumn Osso Buco
Veal Scaloppine Mary Etta
Chef Ron Barber's Vitella Nordbicciana

SALADS:

A Salad of Coddled Chicken and Finnocchio
Insalata di Puntette e Pignoli (Puntette Pasta and Pine Nut Salad)

A SANDWICH AND A BREAD:

Focaccia Cheese Sandwich

VEGETABLES:

The North Beach Stir-Fry
Spaghetti Squash

DESSERTS:

Chef Edgar Rojas' Fried Cream
Baked Stuffed Pears

ANTIPASTI

GARDINIERE ALLO TONNATO

A sweet and sour antipasto of vegetables and tuna in a tomato-flavored marinade

YIELD: 1½ quarts

Marinade:

- **1 cup white onion in small dice**
- **3 plump cloves garlic, minced**
- **1½ cups fruity olive oil**
- **10 oz. drained, seeded pulp of pear tomatoes**
- **2 level Tbsp tomato paste**

In a large, heavy, enameled pan, melt onion and garlic in oil until soft. Lay tomato pulp on towel to absorb moisture, then crush in a bowl and add to onion mixture. Stir in tomato paste and simmer, uncovered, for 12 minutes. Remove pan from heat.

Vegetables:

- **4 oz. raw carrot, cut with a serrated knife into ¼-inch slices**
- **4 oz. raw cauliflowerettes**
- **4 oz. raw celery or fennel, cut into ¼-inch slices**
- **8 oz. drained canned button mushrooms**
- **4 oz. pitted medium ripe olives, whole**
- **4 oz. giant green olives, bone-in**
- **4 oz. pickled pearl onions, whole**
- **4 oz. serrated thick-cut bread and butter pickles**
- **two 7-oz. fresh tuna steaks or a 13-oz. can of solid-packed tuna**
- **4 oz. roasted red bell pepper**

Briefly steam serrated-cut carrot and cauliflowerettes till crisply *al dente*. Fold into marinade. Fold raw celery into marinade, followed by mushrooms, pickles, onion, and olives.

Tonnato:

Poach the fresh tuna steaks about 5 minutes. If fresh tuna is unavailable, use a 13-oz. can of solid-packed albacore tuna, packed in water. (I stipulate the 13-oz. can as the chunks will be larger than with two 7-oz. cans, and the tuna will continue to chunk as you remove it from the can and fold it into the marinade. You want to keep the pieces as large as possible so that you have big bites rather than flakes.) Have ready the roasted red bell pepper, which is folded gently—along with the tuna—into the marinade. Refrigerate overnight. Bring to room temperature before serving.

NOTE:

You may substitute artichoke hearts for mushrooms, French-cut raw green beans for celery, eggplant for mushroms. All ingredients should be coated with marinade, not swimming in it. This may be frozen in airtight containers, or canned by bringing to boil and sealing in sterilized containers. In most Italian households, this is served with a small glass of slightly chilled vermouth (try Lillet brand) with a lemon twist.

NORTH BEACH FISHERMAN'S SALAD

YIELD: 4 entrée portions, or 6 antipasti

8 oz. cleaned calamari (baby squid), about 1 lb. before cleaning (see note below)

8 oz. medium-size sea scallops

Cut the cleaned squid into thin rings. Cut these rings of tentacles in half if they are large. Cut scallops into same size strips as calamari rings. Holding squid in a strainer, colander, or towel, lower them into simmering water for the count of 15; lift them out the instant they whiten—before they become tough. Dip into cold water, then towel dry. Combine with the raw scallop strips.

Marinade:

1 cup thinly sliced celery

¼ cup thinly sliced sweet onion

6 thinly sliced green onions

2 Tbsp minced parsley

1 Tbsp minced oregano (or ½ tsp dried)

1/3 cup olive oil

¼ tsp black pepper grindings

Up to ¼ cup white wine vinegar, added a little at a time, till tart enough

Combine marinade ingredients, add fish and marinate in refrigerator at least two hours, or overnight. Bring to room temperature before serving on bed of shredded lettuce.

NOTE:

To clean calamari, pull out head and tentacles, cut off tentacles above eyes, and pop out the hard little round bitter-tasting mouth, located in center of tentacles. Working under cold running water, loosen strip of plastic spine and pull it out of body, squeezing and washing away all the insides and rubbing off the skin.

BASIL

PESTO BASE ALLA WASHINGTON SQUARE BAR & GRILL: A NORTH BEACH SECRET

Essence of well-flavored sweet basil, prepared in summertime
for year-round use

YIELD: 1 pint

**5 bunches sweet basil
  (use leaves and flow-
  ers, but never stems)**
**2 Tbsp minced leaves of
  Italian flat-leafed
  parsley (optional)**
4 peeled cloves garlic
½ cup (4 oz.) olive oil

Put through food processor or blender, some of each ingredient at a time, until the entire batch is processed. If you seem to need more than ½-cup of oil to mascerate the basil (which will depend upon the fullness of the bunches), add it sparingly.

Run processor or blender a little longer just until the mixture is smooth and pasty, but no longer. Store mixture in small Tupperware or other good-quality plastic containers with tight-fitting lids. Store portion for immediate use in a glass jar in the refrigerator, where it will hold flavoring oils for a couple of months. For longer storage (up to nine months), use the freezer.

Recipes for using this pesto base follow. They include two pesto sauces, a basil-flavored pasta, basil butter, sweet basil vinegar, a vegetarian pasta and lentil casserole, and a cheese fantasy. See the **EGGS** section for the omelette made with this purée.

NOTE:
See "Basilico" in **Glossary** for more information on uses.

PASTA AL PESTO, NORTH BEACH STYLE

YIELD: 6 servings

The order of steps presented below is essential to the proper execution of this dish. Step #5 is the good Italian chef's secret for the perfectly cheesed pasta.

3 oz. pesto base (see preceding recipe)
2 oz. pine nuts
2 oz. half-and-half or light cream
1 oz. heavy cream
2 oz. unsalted butter
salt to taste
OPTIONAL: 1 tsp chicken glaze
1 lb. spinach linguine or pesto-flavored pasta (see recipe, page 106)
8 qts. water, 1Tbsp each, salt and olive oil
2 oz. half-and-half
1 oz. heavy cream
4 oz. unsalted butter, softened
6 oz. freshly grated Reggiano Parmigiano cheese
2 oz. pine nuts, sautéed in butter

STEP #1: Combine pesto base with the next five ingredients (as well as optional sixth), in food processor or blender. Blend until smooth and pasty.

STEP #2: Bring 8 quarts of water to boil. NOW add to the water 1 Tbsp olive oil and 1 Tbsp salt. Add pasta slowly so as not to interrupt boiling. With a cup of cold water ready, start checking pasta after 3 minutes to see if it is *al dente*. Turn off heat, add cup of cold water, and drain water at once. Do not rinse the pasta.

STEP #3: Put pasta into heated bowl containing 4 oz. softened butter, and toss pasta until coated with butter. Proceeding rapidly:

STEP #4:In a big wide skillet, have ready the light and heavy creams, which have been heated briskly until reduced and thickening, with bubbles starting to appear. Add the pesto sauce from Step #1, and blend it into the creams. Add the buttered pasta, toss over low heat until pasta is coated with, and has absorbed most of, the sauce.

STEP #5: Remove pan from heat. NOW add grated cheese, and toss pasta until every strand is cheese-coated.

STEP #6: Serve pasta in heated bowls, garnished with a sprinkle of pine nuts lightly sautéed in butter.

NOTE:

To make the well-known southern Italian version using our pesto base, just add olive oil and ground pine nuts to the base, and coat the boiled pasta with it. Then proceed to Step #5.

QUADRATTI DI BASILICO

Chef Marcello Persi's invention: strips of sweet-basil-flavored pasta

YIELD: 8 servings

An expert pasta maker can hand-cut this soft dough into noodles, but Chef Persi shows small strips for the novice. If you have one of the great new pasta machines that mix and cut noodles as well as macaroni shapes, this purée-flavored pasta will be such fun to make, with your new toy!

2 whole eggs, beaten into

3 Tbsp pesto base (see recipe page 104)

1¼ lbs. mixed flour (half all-purpose, half semolina, the flour milled from hard winter wheat)

Mix the two flours in the bowl of a processor or electric mixer. Beat two whole eggs into the pesto base, blending thoroughly. Add this mixture to the flours and process until a ball of dough forms. If more flour is needed, sprinkle it in.

Remove the dough to a floured board, cover it with a cloth or inverted bowl, and let it rest one hour.

Knead the dough, working in a little more all-purpose flour as you fold, push, press, and turn—repeating this for about 10 minutes or until dough is smooth and non-sticky. (It will be softer than unflavored pasta dough.)

Cut the dough into fourths. Roll each fourth out into a thin sheet. If sheet becomes sticky during rolling, sprinkle on all-purpose flour, roll it up like a jelly roll, lay it down and open it up to the other side, sprinkle flour on that side, and continue rolling. When thin enough, cut the sheets into bias strips one-inch by two-inches long. Lay out in one layer on tea towels.

If you are not cooking all the pasta at once, have ready a shallow-lidded box (like the box ravioli comes in or a cake box), and some rice flour (from an Italian delicatessen), and waxpaper sheets cut to fit inside the boxes. Sprinkle cut pieces with rice flour to prevent them from sticking to each other, and lay them out inside the box in layers separated by waxpaper. Freeze them until ready to use.

To cook the pasta, bring 8 quarts water to a rolling boil, THEN add 1 Tbsp olive oil and 1 Tbsp salt, then pasta strips, a few at a time (so as not to disturb the boil), and cook about 3 minutes or until *al dente*. Drain, but do not rinse.

Continue from Step #3, in the pasta al pesto recipe, page 105.

NOTE:

This dough can be used as skins, to fill with your favorite cheese filling for ravioli, manicotti, or any filled pasta.

SWEET BASIL VINEGAR

1 quart pear vinegar
1 bunch fresh basil, in
   season

Remove roots and wash the basil clean of soil and sand. Remove any yellowed leaves and push the basil stalks down into a crock or glass container with a large mouth.

Bring vinegar to a boil and immediately pour it over the basil. Allow the vinegar to cool and then cover it. Store it in a dark cool place for about ten days. Strain the vinegar into a scalded wine bottle and cork it tightly.

SOME SUGGESTIONS FOR USE: This makes a fine dieter's salad dressing, as is. It is excellent sprinkled lightly over raw fish or it can be combined with a light olive oil to dress tomatoes or salads. (This works best with very little oil. For a lovely sweet basil vinaigrette, add plain pear vinegar to some of the pesto base, with more olive oil.) Use it also to deglaze the sauté pan next time you sauté strips of calves liver, boned chicken, or rabbit. Sweet basil vinegar is also used in the Cheese Fantasy recipe on page 109.

CONCHIGLIETTE E LENTICCHE AL PESTO

Tiny pasta shells with lentils, pesto, and cheese

YIELD: 6 servings

This dish is a balanced protein entrée, for meatless days. If soy margarine and tofu cheese are substituted for the dairy products, the dish will contain no animal products.

1 12-oz. package of dried lentils
1 qt. water
1 tsp salt
1 cup tomato purée
2 cups peeled, seeded, and chopped tomatoes
3 cloves garlic
1 tsp honey
4 Tbsp basil butter (see page 109)
1 Tbsp plus 1 tsp pesto base (see page 104)
4 tsp grated cheese
¼ cup minced parsley
7 oz. conchigliette (tiny pasta shells)
6 very thin slices of Bel Paese cheese

Wash the beans and pick out any stones. Cover the beans with water, add salt, and simmer gently, covered, for 15 minutes or until just tender. (The lentils should still hold their shape. Watch them closely so they don't mush.) Remove from the heat. Do not drain.

Add tomatoes and purée, honey and garlic-through-the-press. Cook another 15 minutes, uncovered. Fold in the sweet basil butter and the pesto base, then the grated cheese and the minced parsley.

Fold in the tiny shells, which you will have cooked briefly, until slightly less than *al dente*. (A shell cut in half should show a little white.) Pour into buttered individual shallow gratinée casseroles, cover with thin slices of cheese, and bake in 350° oven about 5 minutes, until the cheese bubbles.

SWEET BASIL BUTTER

1 cup pesto base (see
 page 104)
½ Tbsp concentrated
 lemon juice (from
 about 1½ Tbsp fresh
 lemon juice, reduced
 over high heat until
 syrupy, and cooled
 before using)
½ tsp salt
1 cup softened unsalted
 butter

Blend into a smooth paste. Shape into long round logs, one inch in diameter, on sheets of waxpaper. Roll the butter logs in waxpaper and freeze them. A log will slice easily into pats while still frozen, enabling you to use it as you need it, without thawing more than you need.

SOME SUGGESTIONS FOR USE: Serve sliced on grilled fish or poultry, or in a baked potato, or on steamed vegetables, rice, or pasta. Butter bread with it for a sandwich of sweet onion, cheese, and tomato. Fold it into eggs while scrambling. Use it to stuff your next Chicken Kiev.

SWEET BASIL CHEESE FANTASY

YIELD: 24 madeleines, or 15 one-ounce molds

This has a whipped cream-cheese center, masked by a light coating of pale green sweet-basil-flavored aspic. Use it as a garnish, or to complement a cheese plate entrée, or as a light luncheon appetizer or salad, or for the buffet table. We prefer molding the fantasies in a madeleine plaque, but any small mold (or even a pie tin) would do.

Basil Infusion:
1 cup loosely packed
 basil leaves and
 flowerbuds (no stems)
1 cup water

Use your fingers to tear the basil into the cup of cold water in the bottom of a Pyrex double boiler. Mash the basil into the water with a glass, marble or wood instrument (do not use metal). Bring to a boil, lower heat to simmer as soon as

the mixture bubbles, count to twenty-five, and remove it from the heat. Let it sit until it cools. Following these instructions carefully will prevent the basil oils from turning bitter. Strain into a glass container. This infusion will keep its flavor in the refrigerator for a month.

Cheese Fantasy:

¾ Tbsp plain gelatin

3 oz. basil infusion (see directions)

6 oz. unsweetened pineapple juice

3 level Tbsp sugar

¼ tsp salt

1 ½ oz. sweet basil vinegar (see page 107)

4 oz. fresh cream cheese at room temperature

1 Tbsp cold heavy cream

Pour gelatin into a 16-oz. measuring cup. Add the basil infusion to soften the gelatin. Bring pineapple juice to boil and then stir it in to dissolve the gelatin. Add the sugar, salt, and vinegar. Place the mixture in the refrigerator until it thickens slightly and will coat spoon. (This should take about 10 minutes.) Run cold water over the molds to moisten them and then spoon just enough aspic to thinly coat the inside surfaces of the mold, and refrigerate about 15 minutes.

Whip the cream with the softened cream cheese. Spoon a little cheese into molds, and return to the fridge. Now return the rest of the unused aspic to the refrigerator for about 10 minutes or until it is thick enough to adhere to the top of the cheese filling. Spoon aspic over cheese and smooth it out. The aspic will be tough enough to handle with ease. Refrigerate until ready to unmold and serve. Just wipe bottom of molds with hot towel to unmold. The unmolded Fantasies will hold up very well on a buffet table.

NOTE:

If you have no basil vinegar, use fresh lime juice with a vinegar made from honey, sake, or sherry, blended to your taste, to total 1½ oz.

SOUP

CHEF ALDO PERSICH'S MINESTRONE

YIELD: 4 quarts

2 cups dry cranberry
beans
A ham bone, or piece of
prosciutto bone, or
the skin, fat, and
bone of a ham, tied
into a bundle.
1 Tbsp back fat*
1½ stalks leeks
1 large white onion
¼ head celery
½ head medium or ¼
head large Savoy
curly cabbage (don't
use regular cabbage
for this)
1 lb.-12 oz. can whole
pear tomatoes in juice
from 1½ to 2 pints rich
chicken stock
freshly ground pepper
2 medium carrots (no
more)
1 lb. Italian green beans
OR 4 medium
zucchini (not both)
1 large potato (no more)
2 oz. Ave Maria or other
small pasta for soup)
Parmigiano, Asiago, or
Locatelli cheese

Put picked-over and washed beans into soaking pot with the ham bone. Cover the beans and bones with water twice their volume, and soak overnight in the refrigerator. Drain off the soaking water, replace with fresh water to cover, bring to a simmer, and cook gently about 50 minutes until the beans are tender. Older beans will take longer.

All the vegetables should be chopped to the same size, about ¼-inch dice. To clean the leek, chop it first, then wash it in a strainer to rid it of sand. Chop the onion and celery, and core and chop the cabbage. Grind up 1 Tbsp back fat and melt in a 4 qt. stockpot. Add chopped vegetables to the melted fat and cook gently until the onion is transparent, about 8 minutes. Put the tomatoes through a sieve and then add them to the pot. Cook 10 minutes. Add the bean liquor. (Discard the ham skin, fat and bones.) Put half the cooked beans into a stockpot. In a food processor, process the other half *briefly* or put them through a meat grinder equipped with the fine plate, without pushing. (Don't push them through, nor process long, as they musn't get mushy.) Grinding half the beans gives minestrone its characteristic texture. Add the loosely ground beans to the pot. Add 1½ pts chicken broth, more if ground beans soak up too much liquid. Add pepper grindings to taste, but no salt. Add raw carrots, beans or squash, and potato, all cut into ¼-inch dice, and cook until the vegetables are tender.

If serving the entire batch at one sitting, add all the soup pasta. If some soup is to be reserved for later, separate it before adding the proportionate amount of pasta, which should always be added at the last minute to prevent the leftover soup from souring. After adding the pasta, stir it in, cover the pot tightly, turn off the heat and let the pasta cook from the heat of the soup.

Grate cheese over the filled serving bowls.

*NOTE:

Back fat can be purchased from R. Iacopi & Son; see page 85.

PASTA, POTATO, AND RICE

RISSOTO DI PUNTETTE

A rissoto made with a rice-grain-shaped pasta

YIELD: 4 to 6 servings

1 Tbsp each butter and olive oil
2 small white onions
1 plump garlic clove
8 oz. puntette
15 oz. chicken stock, boiling

Bring butter and oil to heat in a heavy pan with a tight-fitting lid, and sauté minced onion and garlic until soft. Add the pasta and sauté until coated. Add the boiling stock and, as soon as the stock returns to a boil, cover the pan tightly and do not uncover it until done. (Regulate the heat so covered pasta does not boil over, moving the pan off-center on the burner, if need be, now and then.) Simmer for a total of 10 minutes, and immediately move the still-covered pan to a cold back burner, to sit undisturbed for half an hour, or until pasta absorbs all the liquid and becomes creamy and ready to serve. If the pasta sits much longer than 45 minutes, you may want to slowly bring the pan to heat again. Stir in bits of whole butter to enrich it if you wish. If you're splurging on saffron, now's the time to add it, dissolved in a little stock. Also, it's time to stir in grated cheese, if you like, minced parsley, and/or sautéed mushrooms.

NOTE:

In North Beach shops, Eduardo's excellent egg pasta comes in a melon-seed shape that works well for this recipe.

FETTUCCINE CHEF BARDELLI

These cooks, they play musical chairs, hopping from one restaurant to another, learning and forgetting and recalling again an oral history of the food preparations of their experience. Chef Scott Leary is responsible for the survival of this recipe, suddenly remembering it one day, many years after Chef Bardelli and the establishment bearing his name had forgotten it.

YIELD: 4 to 6 portions

1 lb. fettuccine
8 qts. water, olive oil, and salt
¼ lb butter
1 oz. prosciutto fat
1 cup thin-sliced mushrooms
4 minced shallots
salt and pepper
4 oz. heavy cream
up to 4 oz. Sauce Napoletana (see below)
4 oz. grated Reggiano Parmagiano cheese

Cook pasta *al dente*. Drain, do not rinse. Sauté prosciutto fat in the butter until crisp, add the shallots and sauté until they are soft, add mushrooms and sauté briefly. Grind in salt and pepper to taste.*

Add the heavy cream and heat until the cream bubbles. Add Sauce Napoletana to the cream mixture, a spoonful at a time, tasting, until the proportion of tomato to cream suits your palate. If the mushrooms produced liquid, simmer the sauce until it's thick enough to coat the pasta. Working quickly, add the drained hot pasta to the sauce, tossing gently until sauce is absorbed. Off-heat, toss pasta with grated cheese until every strand is cheese-coated.

*Starting with this step, the chafing dish virtuoso can work in the dining room.

SAUCE NAPOLETANA

(Basic Tomato Sauce)

YIELD: about 1 quart

1 plump garlic clove
one 1-lb., 12 oz. can
    whole pear tomato
    in purée
3 tsp olive oil
1 tsp salt
ground pepper
1 small onion
1 small carrot
1 lower rib of celery
parsley stems (no leaves)
a pinch of sugar

Select a heavy enameled iron pan or a stainless steel pan. Crush the unpeeled garlic with the flat of a knife and brown it in the olive oil. Discard the garlic. Over a bowl, halve the tomatoes to scrape out their bitter-tasting seeds. Pour the contents of the can into the pan, and then strain the liquids into the pan. Coarsely chop the tomatoes and add to the pan, along with the chopped onion, carrot, and parsley stems. Add the salt, pepper, and sugar. (Yes, sugar—it acts chemically to develop the flavor of the tomatoes.) Bring the mixture to a boil, lower the heat, cover, and simmer for about 20 minutes. Uncover and simmer, stirring, for another 15 minutes or until the tomatoes lose their acidity and the liquids reduce. Pass the sauce through a food mill or a coarse sieve. (Don't use a food processor as it robs the sauce of its texture.) This sauce may be frozen.

CHEF STELVIO STORACHE'S POTATO GNOCCHI

YIELD: 6 portions

4 baked potatoes, 9 to
    10 oz. each
2 tsp butter
1 egg yolk
1 ⅛ cups flour

Baking the potatoes makes the big difference in Chef Stelvio's famous gnocchi. Scoop out the soft baked flesh from the potatoes, add the remaining ingredients, and knead into a dough. On a lightly floured surface, roll dough into finger-thick rolls the size of breadsticks. Cut into ¾-inch lengths, cook in boiling salted water until they rise to the surface, and remove with a slotted spoon. Toss with melted butter and grated Parmesan cheese. Serve with a saucy braised-beef dish, or a creamy pesto sauce. Uncooked portion of the cut gnocchi may be frozen for later use.

CHEF ALDO'S WILD RICE

Chef Aldo's simple method of preparing wild rice reveals the subtle taste and texture of this unique grain.

YIELD: 2 to 3 servings

4 Tbsp (2 oz.) rinsed wild rice
6 oz. cold water
1 Tbsp butter
salt and pepper to taste
2 oz. prosciutto, or other good ham, diced
4 sliced green onions, including the tops

Run water over the rice in a strainer. Put the 4 Tbsp wild rice into a pan with 6 oz. cold water, cover tightly, bring to simmer, simmer slowly for about 8 minutes, and remove to a 200° warming oven or a warmer tray, to sit undisturbed for 45 minutes until the grains of rice have exploded, like popcorn.

Save any leftover liquid for broths or baking. Over medium heat, melt the butter, toss ham, add drained rice and sliced onions and toss to coat. Taste for salt (the ham may add enough) and grind in pepper to taste.

EGGS

ARTICHOKE FRITTATA

YIELD: Will serve 4 to 12, depending upon its role in the meal

2½ dozen baby globe artichokes, 1 to 2 inches in diameter before peeling
¾ of a big sweet onion*
2 garlic cloves
1 Tbsp olive oil, as well as a little butter
8 eggs, beaten lightly (don't beat too much air into them)
freshly ground pepper

To prepare the artichokes, strip away the outer leaves until the artichokes are the size of giant olives. Whack off the prickly tip, and lightly trim the stem ends.

Slice the onion paper thin. Sauté the artichokes with the onion in just enough oil to do the job without leaving an oily residue. Add a few drops of water to the pan and cover it; lower the flame. After 5 minutes, add the garlic through a press, and continue cooking until the artichokes and onions are tender—about 15 minutes in all, depending on the starting size of the artichokes before peeling, and how long it has been since they were picked. The dish can be done ahead up to this point and refrigerated. Bring it back to room temperature before making the frittata.

Preheat the oven to 325° Bring the artichoke-onion mixture to heat, pour the lightly beaten eggs over the artichokes, grind in some pepper, stir around in the pan and cook over low heat just to set the bottom. Then bake in the oven from 15 to 25 minutes, until the top is set. Serve hot, or cool to room temperature.

NOTE:

Salt is optional, but any other herb or spice added to this dish will detract from the subtle flavor of the artichokes.

*In the Bay Area, Walla Walla sweet onions are in season during baby artichoke season.

THE VEGETARIAN JOE'S SPECIAL

The meatless Joe was born one night when a hungry Zen author asked Chef Ron Barber to toss together in a pan anything he could find that looked vegetarian.

YIELD: 1 serving

2 Tbsp chopped onion
1 clove pressed garlic
oil or butter, as needed
4 oz. (½ cup) wilted spinach, squeezed quite dry and chopped fine
3 eggs*
an herb to taste
ground pepper
salt, or tamari
1 cup vegetables (see list below)

This is a loosely scrambled egg dish. Sauté onion and garlic in an egg pan. Mix in the spinach. Season the eggs and beat lightly, add spinach mixture and toss, add vegetables and toss. Return to pan and cook gently, scrambling with fork until everything is egg-coated and egg is lightly set.

VEGETABLE SUGGESTIONS: Asparagus; any summer squash; sugar snap peas; bell peppers; sprouted seeds; sautéed Chinese long beans with cilantro; steamed spaghetti squash with cherry tomatoes, basil, and grated cheese.

JOE'S SPECIAL: To make a regular Joe, stir-sauté 4 oz. ground beef with onion, and omit the cup of vegetables.

*Tofu can be substituted for eggs.

NORTH BEACH OMELETTE

YIELD: 1 portion

2 Tbsp (1 oz.) diced baked ham
1 Tbsp pesto base (see page 104)
3 eggs
1 Tbsp butter
2 heaping Tbsp whole-milk ricotta cheese, at room temperature
freshly ground pepper
salt

Beat eggs a few strokes, add the pesto base and ham, and the salt and pepper to taste, and beat just enough to combine.

Melt butter in a hot egg pan, pour in the egg mixture. Just before folding into a French-style omelette, add ricotta cheese to center of omelette. Hold the folded omelette at the edge of the pan a few seconds before turning out onto a hot plate.

FISH

ITALO LUCCHESI'S BACCALA FRITTERS

For all of us Northbeachniks for whom a stop at Italo's counter at the old Buon Gusto for one of these sweet little devils was, for many years, a Friday ritual, here's a present:

YIELD: 6 to 12 servings, depending upon its role in the meal

HOW TO SELECT A DRIED COD: The Italian-style whole butterflied baccala is available in North Beach at Florence and Panelli delicatessens. Some of that dried fish is skate, not cod, so always ask to be sure you get cod. To select, look for meaty thickness at the center. Some of them are too bony to be worth all the trouble. The yield required by this recipe, after hydration, is only 10 to 12 ounces. The clerks at both shops will be able to estimate the cooked yield.

HOW TO PREPARE DRIED COD FOR COOKING: Use your deepest basin or bucket, to hold the maximum of cold water. (You'll have to change the water more often in smaller vessels to extract the salt. Change it as often as you can. Use a deep laundry sink, or leave it overnight in the bathtub.) Immerse the cod, whether boxed salt-cod fillets or the whole beast, from 8 to 10 hours, until the fish is plump and has lost its saltiness. Peel the skin off, bring it to a boil in a large covered pan full of fresh water. Cook it 3 to 4 minutes; turn off heat and let it stand 5 minutes. Drain and cool. Bone it, feeling every little piece for small bones. Pull the boned flesh into shreds.

FRITTERS

2 eggs
6 oz. flour
½ tsp baking powder
up to 4 oz. milk to
    make a batter thick
    enough to bind the
    cod
10 to 12 oz. boned and
    shredded cod

Beat the first four ingredients together into a thickish batter. Add the shreds of cod and mix well. Use a tablespoon to spoon the mixture out into very hot oil, in a pan or on a grill. Press to flatten, and cook both sides until golden. Have ready a shallow casserole with a coat of sauce (see below) in the bottom. Lay the fritters, as cooked, atop the sauce and, when all fritters are done, spoon another coat of sauce on top. You can hold it all warm on a warming tray or in a warming oven. The fritters are also good at room temperature.

ITALO'S TOMATO SAUCE

3 Tbsp olive oil
white of one small leek,
    coarsely chopped
2 one-inch boiling
    onions, coarsely
    chopped
1 plump clove
    garlic, minced
a few grains of sugar
2 cups plum tomato in
    purée
2 cups water
¼ cup minced parsley

Sauté the onions, garlic, and leek in oil until soft. Add the tomato and water, cook down about 30 minutes, or until tomatoes lose their acidity and the sauce is sweet. Put through food mill or coarse sieve. Stir in the parsley.

CHEF MANUEL SAUSEDO'S CRAB CIOPPINO AND POLENTA

The North Beach chef's secret to a proper cioppino is to dissect the crab alive, and to so cut each leg that the section of body from which it protrudes is left attached to the leg. These two steps keep the crab juicy during sautéing, and give the stew the intense crab flavor that makes this so different from other fish stews.

Crab season opens in early October in the state of Washington, and their Dungeness come in almost twice the size of ours, but they come in already cooked. San Francisco fishermen go out for crab starting the second Tuesday in November. Eureka starts trucking crab down on December first. The crabs are so out of gas from the long trip that the fishmongers cook them at once. Your best shot at finding live crabs at the Stockton Street Chinese fishmarkets is between November 2 and December 1. (Crabs begin to peter out in February and March.)

YIELD: 6 servings

2 Dungeness crabs, live
2 oz. corn oil
2 garlic cloves, minced
1 medium white onion, finely chopped
½ small green bell pepper, minced
12 clams in shell
12 large prawns, cleaned
12 2-inch chunks of rock cod
6 oz. dry white wine
6 oz. clam juice
2 cups pear tomatoes, drained
⅛ of the shell of a chili pequino (dried)

Lay the crabs on their backs on a table, and, with one whack of a sharp cleaver, bissect them from head to tail. This dispatches them more quickly than throwing them into boiling water, which will also detract from their flavor. Remove the back shell and the gray fibrous matter. (Do this over a bowl to catch all the yellow-orange stuff and white crab fat, with which you will flavor the stew.) Then separate the claws and legs so that each leg is still attached to its adjoining body section. Lightly crack the leg shells and claws.

In large sautoir, melt the garlic, onion, and green pepper in the corn oil. Add the crab sections and sauté very briefly until the crab begins to take on color. Add the clams, prawns, and rock cod. (Do not substitute for the rock cod, because it is its disintegration in the stew that gives it the characteristic gelatinous texture.) Coat all fish with the onion mixture. Put drained tomatoes through a food mill or a coarse sieve (don't process, or they'll lose the needed texture), crumble the chili shell, and add both, along with the yellow-orange stuff and white crab fat which we caught in a bowl, the wine and clam juice. Cook 12 cooked polenta (see below), with cocktail forks and crab bibs to assist the diners.

SOFT-COOKED POLENTA

YIELD: 6 servings

1 cup polenta (fine corn meal)
5 cups water
1 Tbsp chicken-stock base
2 oz. butter

Bring 2½ cups of the water to a rolling boil. Dissolve the chicken base and butter in the boiling water. Quickly stir the cornmeal into the other 2½ cups of cold water, and then gradually add the cornmeal mixture to the boiling water. When the full boil resumes,

lower the heat and simmer uncovered for about 40 minutes, stirring very frequently to prevent sticking. (You can use your grilltop to simmer the polenta, if you need to free space for the stewpot.) The polenta's ready to serve as soon as it's thick, smooth, and creamy. If it must wait a few minutes, someone will have to keep stirring it.

Start the polenta before you start the stewpot, to bring them to the ready simultaneously. If you can't manage both preparations at once, make the polenta ahead and pour the cooked polenta into a buttered shallow lasagne-type pan, to harden and be cut into squares. (But soft polenta is so good with these fish stews! I suppose the combination began back when every kitchen had a *nonna*—grandmother—helping in it.)

BEEF

CHEF JOHN MARCONCINI'S CULOTTE STEAK

The culotte is another of the rich, intensely beefy-tasting, lesser-known steaks the butcher takes home with him. Know your butcher when you special-order it, as the culotte has a tough twin. The "triangle tip of the bottom sirloin" is its right name, so specify. (It's lookalike comes from the bottom round, and is not tender.)

The culotte varies in size, tasting best from the largest, prime ox. It's a fairly tender, triangle-shaped, very-well-marbled muscle, topped with a slab of fat that looks like a diaper—hence its name. (Culotte is French slang meaning "britches"; Marie Antoinette called the rabblerousers the *sans-culotte*, running around down there, club in hand, wearing nothing but their long shirts.) A good-sized culotte will yield from two to three 12-oz. individual steaks. To get even-sized portions from a triangle shape, the butcher will trim the ends of the muscle, cut out the steaks at an angle, give the top fat an "apache" trim, and cut the meat away from its strip of fat, punching it down into long steak shapes which can be dry-cooked in a pan or over coals. If grilling more than one in a pan, don't let them touch each other during cooking. Grill the steaks fat side down in a hot dry pan. After fat has rendered enough to film the pan, remove fat strips and brown all over, working quickly from start to finish, over high heat, so the meat does not overcook. Slightly undercook before adding sauce ingredients (see below) directly into the pan with the steaks (or, you can produce a show in a chafing dish).

CULOTTE STEAK SAUCE (per portion)

2 oz. butter	Poke steak all over with fork while
½ Tbsp Dijon mustard	swishing it around, over lowered heat,
½ Tbsp paprika	in butter and seasonings, until the sauce
¼ tsp Lea & Perrins	is well blended, reduced, and absorbed
Worcestershire Sauce	into the steak enough to glaze it all over.
freshly ground pepper	Pour any extra sauce over the steak.
juice of half a lemon	Serve with cottage fries or Potatoes Anna.

NOTE:

If you're deft at the brazier, you can grill the culotte whole, as Chef John does, and slice it into wide slabs after saucing, for a different texture, with less of the glazed browned outer surfaces of the individually grilled steaks. The culotte sauce ingredients can also be combined in a food processor and rolled in wax-paper logs for the freezer, to use as a handy compound butter for other steaks.

CHICKEN

CHEF SILVIO CONCIATORE'S CHICKEN JERUSALEM WITH BABY ARTICHOKES

YIELD: 4 portions

**two 2½-lb. broiler
  chickens, disjointed**
2 Tbsp butter
2 Tbsp olive oil
1½ cups chopped onion
4 garlic cloves, minced
6 oz. sweet sherry
6 oz. rich chicken stock
**baby artichokes
  (see note)**
8 oz. fresh mushrooms
**¾ cup Besciamella
  Sauce (see below)**
salt
freshly ground pepper

Melt the butter and oil in a heavy pan. Sprinkle the chicken pieces with salt and pepper and, putting no more in pan at once than can lie side-by-side without overlapping, brown the chicken. Hold off heat as they brown, and when all pieces are removed, sauté the onion and garlic in the pan until delicately colored. Return the chicken to pan, add the sherry, raise the heat and bubble the wine uncovered for 5 minutes. Add the chicken stock, cover, lower the heat and simmer 10 minutes. Add the artichokes, cover, and cook 8 minutes. Use the mushrooms whole if small; halve or quarter if larger. Fold the mushrooms into the pan, cooking 8 minutes more or until the chicken and chokes are tender. Uncover and cook a few minutes longer until the pan juices are reduced. Fold in Besciamella Sauce and serve.

NOTE:

You'll want about one-and-a-half dozen baby artichokes if they are 1 inch in diameter, eight if they are 2 inches wide, six if 2½ wide. If under 2 inches, use them whole; halve if 2 inches wide. If larger than 2 inches, cut into thirds and there will be some fuzz to cut out at the choke. This recipe doesn't work with artichokes larger than 2½ inches. See **Artichoke Frittata**, page 117, for trimming instruction.

BESCIAMELLA SAUCE

1 Tbsp butter
1 Tbsp flour
1 cup milk
salt
white pepper

Melt the butter in the top of a double boiler. Stir in flour and cook, stirring for 5 minutes. Pour in the milk, beat until smooth. Raise the heat and beat until it boils. Add a little salt. Simmer over low heat for about 30 minutes, stirring as necessary to prevent sticking. When the sauce is thick enough to coat a spoon, add a little white pepper. Beat until smooth before folding into the completed chicken.

CHEF TULLIO ROSATI'S FILETTI DI POLLO ALLA FONTINA

Fontina cheese-crusted baked breast of chicken

YIELD: 4 servings

And to those who mourn that our North Beach cooking style is disappearing with the old-time chefs, we happily point out the young cooks who grew up here and have learned under the tutelage of the *capi di cucina*, as well as the newcomers still arriving from Italy—young cooks who care very much about incorporating our ways with food into their own training. Tullio Rosati is a *bobsledder*! from the town of Ovindoli in the district of L'Aquila, the winter sports center inland from Rome, and he's fearlessly competent at the range as well.

2 1-lb. boned chicken breasts*
4 oz. chopped shallots
6 oz. chopped onion
2 oz. butter
¾ cup fresh bread crumbs**
8 oz. Fontina D'Aosta cheese
4 oz. veal or chicken stock
4 oz. dry vermouth
1½ oz. butter, cut in-to bits

Preheat oven to 325°. Sauté shallots and onions in butter until soft. Spoon half the onion mixture into four individual gratinée casseroles, lightly buttered. Have the chicken breasts ready—boned, skinned, halved, salted, and peppered. Lay a half breast atop the onion in each casserole, and spoon the other half of the onion mixture over the breasts.

Remove crusts from the fresh bread before briefly crumbing it in a processor or blender. Fontina D'Aosta is a creamy cheese. Have it *very* cold before cutting it into chunks and very briefly processing it, or it will cream instead of grating. (Or grate the whole piece, while very cold, with a cold hand-grater.) Toss the cheese with crumbs until well mixed, and cover tops of chicken with the mixture. Dot tops with bits of cold butter.

Pour the vermouth into the onion-cooking pan and bring to a boil. Add the veal stock and lower the heat to moderately high to reduce the liquid somewhat. Spoon the reduced liquid into the edges of casseroles, all around the meat. Bake in a 325° oven for 20 minutes, until the chicken is tender, the stock is absorbed, and the top is a golden crust.

*You'll need two 3½- to 3¾-lb. chickens to get two 1-pound breasts, unless your butcher offers parts from large birds.
**Whole-grain bread works best in this dish, and we prefer Italian cornflour bread from Cuneo and Danilo Bakeries (see pages 79 and 80).

CHEF TONY PENADO'S
BORSA DI POLLO PIEMONTESE

Pouches of chicken, stuffed with prosciutto and Piedmont butter,
alla Marsala

YIELD: 4 servings

The son of a chef, Tony got his feel for cooking during his childhood
in Piemonte. When a war injury interrupted his naval engineering
career, he taught himself to cook, settled in North Beach, and established the reputation of three of our town's most famous restaurants.
Now, lame and legally blind, our teaching *capo di cucina* can transform
a talented restaurant apprentice into an able cook faster than a whole
culinary school.

2 1-lb. chicken breasts, boned and skinned*
a few drops of lemon juice
4 paper thin slices of prosciutto ham
flour for dredging
2 whole eggs, lightly beaten
Piedmont butter (see below)
4 rusks or biscotti, finely crumbed
olive oil and butter for sautéing
2 oz. Marsala wine
2 oz. chicken stock
juice of ½ lemon, strained

Between sheets of waxpaper, press the
four half-breasts into ¼-inch-thick
cutlets, using a mallet and a gentle slid-
ing motion. Butterfly each cutlet and
lay out on waxpaper. Squeeze a few
drops of lemon juice over each piece.

On half of each butterflied cutlet, lay
a slice of prosciutto cut to fit. Spread
some of the Piedmont butter down the
center of the other halves. Fold the
buttered halves over the ham-covered
halves, and press the edges to seal.
Dredge the stuffed chicken pouches
with flour, dip in egg, and roll to coat
lightly with the rusk crumbs. Let them
stand awhile to set the coating.

Over medium heat, brown the
pouches in butter and oil until golden
on each side. Set aside and keep warm
while you deglaze the pan with
Marsala, stirring in the cooking bits.

Add boiling stock and lemon juice. Reduce liquid over high heat
until almost syrupy. Lower heat to simmer and return the pouches
to pan. Coat them with sauce on one side and put them sauced-side
down on serving plates. Spoon the remaining sauce over the top
sides.

*You'll need 3½ to 3¾ lbs. chickens to get 1-lb. breasts. If your butcher bones
breasts, order two breasts 10-oz. after boning.

PIEDMONT BUTTER

1 stick (4 oz.) unsalted
   butter
2 heaping Tbsp grated
   Parmesan cheese
grated zest (yellow
   only) of ½ lemon
grated nutmeg

Bring the butter to room temperature.
Blend with cheese, lemon zest, and
nutmeg. (Pass the nutmeg over a grater
three times, or use a tiny pinch of
ground nutmeg.)

NOTE:

You'll have leftover Piedmont butter. Roll it into a log in waxpaper and freeze
it, to slice as needed for finishing sauces for chicken, veal, and vegetables, or to
put in baked potatoes.

PORK

SAM DEITSCH'S FENNEL-ROASTED PORK WITH SAUERKRAUT AND RED CABBAGE

YIELD: 4 servings

3½ to 4 lb. rib-end of
    pork loin, trimmed
    of most of its fat
3 plump cloves of
    garlic, pressed
1 Tbsp. balsamic
    vinegar
1 tsp coarse salt
3 grindings of black
    pepper
1 Tbsp fennel seeds,
    crushed with mortar
    and pestle
2 cups sauerkraut (from
    the grocer's refriger-
    ator section)
3 thin slices of pancetta
    (Italian unsmoked,
    pepper-cured bacon)
    cut into small squares
1 tsp whole fennel seeds
8 scrubbed small new
    potatoes

Wipe the pork joint with a damp cloth. Combine the next five ingredients and rub into all sides of the pork. Let it stand 2 hours at room temperature, or overnight in the refrigerator.

Select an unglazed clay pot to fit the roast. Soak it 15 minutes in cold water. Scrape the marinade off the pork and pat dry with towels. Put sauerkraut into strainer and run cold water well through it. Squeeze the sauerkraut dry with your hands, then squeeze again in a cloth, twisting until it's quite dry. Mix pancetta and whole fennel seeds into the sauerkraut. Remove the bottom of clay pot from water and line it with sauerkraut. Set the pork atop sauerkraut, surrounding it with scrubbed new potatoes. Remove the lid of pot from water and cover the pot. Place in center of cold oven, set heat to 485°, and set timer for 90 minutes. After 90 minutes, insert a microwave instant thermometer into thickest part of the joint, avoiding the bone. It will read 130° when ready. If not, recover the pot and give it up to another 20 minutes. (If you're using a clay pot for the first time, let me caution you that oven mitts are not adequate protection from steam arising when lid is opened. Use two long-handled spatulas to set top askew and allow excess steam to quickly escape, before you get close enough to pick up the lid.)

RED CABBAGE TO ACCOMPANY
PORK AND SAUERKRAUT

This simple red cabbage is a perfect foil to the pork and sauerkraut flavors.

½ **head red cabbage,
  shredded**
juice of ¼ **lemon**
**2 thin slices pancetta,
  cut into small squares**
½ **tsp sugar**
garlic, salt, and pepper
**1 tsp fat (chicken,
  bacon, or roast
  drippings)**

Combine ingredients and braise slowly in a Teflon-coated heavy pan for 30 minutes.

NOTE:

Another good accompaniment to this pork is braised fennel or cardoons (wild artichoke).

VEAL

AN AUTUMN OSSO BUCO

YIELD: 4 servings

veal shanks (8 if using white veal, 4 if rose veal)
1 large red onion, thinly sliced
2 cups unsweetened pineapple juice
grapeseed or olive oil
ground cardamom
flour
3 red bell peppers, cut lengthwise into 1-inch strips
3 ripe tomatoes, peeled, seeded, and juiced
Tie next 3 ingredients in a piece of cheesecloth:
a sprig of oregano (or ½ tsp dried oregano)
a strip lime zest
1 lightly crushed cardamom seed
3 garlic cloves
2 cups veal or chicken stock
2 tsp brown sugar dissolved in 2 Tbsp pineapple juice

Preheat the oven to 325°. Wipe the veal shanks with a damp towel, slit the outer membrane once on each piece, and tie with kitchen twine, to retain shape. Set them in a glass or enameled container to fit, atop a layer of the sliced onion. Cover with the rest of the onion, and pour enough pineapple juice over them to just cover. Marinate two hours. Discard the juice, reserve onions, and rub shanks all over with oil. Return to container, atop a layer of onions, covered with rest of onions, and marinate again, two hours or overnight.

Remove the shanks and reserve the onions. Pat dry. Sprinkle all over with ground cardamom, pat flour into all sides. Select enameled iron casserole large enough to fit all the shanks in a single layer, and cover the bottom with marinade onions.

Film the bottom of a heavy sauté pan with grapeseed oil, bring to sauté heat, and brown the shanks on all sides (avoid having the pieces touch each other in the pan), adding a little oil as needed to keep bottom of pan filmed. Allow 20 minutes for this. Transfer shanks, as browned, to waiting casserole.

Distribute the pepper strips, seasonings, and garlic around and between shanks. Deglaze the sauté pan with stock, scrape sauté essences into the liquid, bring it to a boil, and pour it over veal so that the liquid comes halfway up the sides of the meat. Quarter the tomato flesh and lay over the top of the meat. Sprinkle the pineapple juice and sugar mixture over the tomatoes, lightly cover the meat with foil, cover casserole, bring to simmer and place in 325° oven for 1½ hours, until the meat is ready to fall off of the bone. Scrape aside tomato and remove veal pieces from the casserole, place on hot platter, remove strings, and glaze in 425° oven for 5 minutes, while you boil down casserole juices (after removing cheesecloth bundle) to intensify flavors. Spoon sauce and vegetables over veal, and serve with Rissoto di Puntette (see page 113).

VEAL SCALOPPINE MARY ETTA

Slices of rib eye of veal, sautéed in herb-flavored oil, and glazed with lemon, three cheeses, and Marsala wine

Here's a scaloppine dish that can be served to a dinner party from the limited facilities of the home kitchen. Allow from 1 to 2 hours for the preparation time of the oven-ready casserole, depending upon the number of servings and your own working pace. The oven-ready casserole will wait patiently at room temperature while you take a break.

YIELD: 4 servings

1½ lbs. rib eye of veal, weighed after the "lip"—the long, very narrow strip of meat inside the rib eye—is removed and after the eye is trimmed of all connective tissue and fat
salt and pepper
flour
5 oz. olive oil
several sprigs fresh rosemary, or 1 Tbsp dried rosemary leaves
4 fat garlic cloves, peeled and thinly sliced
2 cold unpeeled small lemons
5 oz. cold Fontina D'Aosta cheese
½ cup veal stock
½ cup dry Marsala
2½ oz. each grated Pecorino Romano and Reggiano Parmigiano cheese
2 oz. (¼ cube) unsalted butter, cold, cut into bits

Save the lip of the rib eye to cube and sauté for a later meal. Cut the rib eye into slices ⅜-inch thick and, with a rolling motion, gently press down on each slice with the flat of a cleaver (don't pound—it's already tender) to flatten it out to ¼-inch thick. Within reach of the stove, lay out sheets of waxpaper long enough to hold all the flattened veal slices. Pat the meat dry, season one side of each slice with salt and pepper, dip both sides in flour and shake off excess, and lay the slices out on the waxpaper.

Discard the ends of lemons, slice lemons *paper thin* while still cold. Halve the slices and lay them out on strips of waxpaper. Discard the seeds. While the cheese is still very cold, use a cheese-parer to slice it very thin, and trim slices to fit within the veal slices. Lay the cheese out on strips of waxpaper. Have the veal, lemon and cheese slices all laid out and coming to room temperature while you prepare the rosemary oil.

Slowly bring oil to heat in heavy sauté pan. Add rosemary sprigs, crushing their oils into the olive oil. When you feel you've extracted their essences, strain oil into cup and discard the herbs.

Return the oil to the pan, bring to heat, add the thinly sliced garlic, and sauté, turning, until the garlic is golden. Strain the oil into a cup, and discard the garlic. (You probably won't need all this oil for this recipe.)

Preheat the oven to 375°. Bring two wide sauté pans to heat. Spoon in just enough of the oil to film the bottom of the pans. Working quickly now, add to each pan just enough scallops to fill pan without having them touch each other during the cooking. Regulate the pan heat to quickly set the flour coating; turn to set other side (about a minute on each side). As soon as each scallop has taken on color, transfer it into a buttered shallow oven casserole, waiting offheat, that is big enough to hold all the scallops—which will slightly overlap during the glazing step. Spoon in more oil as needed to keep pan bottoms filmed during sautéing, till all scallops are golden.

Lay a half-slice of lemon atop each scallop, and a slice of Fontina over each lemon piece. The casserole may be prepared ahead up to this point, foil-covered until ready to glaze, and held at room temperature. (If you can't manage two sauté pans at once, figure twice as long for the blanching step.) Take great care not to cook the meat through during blanching, as the scallops will all be cooked through at once during the oven glazing.

OVEN GLAZING: Bring the sauté pans back to the heat, pour half the Marsala into each pan, and boil down, scraping the cooking essences into the wine. Add the stock, half in each pan, and reduce the liquid just until there is enough to moisten the tops of the veal in the casserole, plus a little extra to moisten the bottom of the casserole. Pour the sauce over the veal and into the casserole at its edges. Sprinkle the combined grated cheeses over all; dot with the bits of cold butter. Place in the upper third of a 375° oven for about 5 minutes, until cheese takes on color and bubbles. Serve at once.

CHEF RON BARBER'S
VITELLA NORDBICCIANA

The North Beach sauté

This is an indigenous North Beach recipe, which appears on the menus peripatetically, as the old-time chefs remember it and then forget it again. Like many good restaurant dishes, this one is prepared— occasionally before your eyes—in a deceptively quick and easy manner. Part of the deception is that half-cup of demi-glacé, the *sine qūa non* of the good restaurant, folded in at the last minute. (You'll need half a day in the kitchen to make an unsalted veal stock to reduce into a glacé, unless you know a chef who moonlights selling demi-glacé.)

Then, there's the technique: it takes a special knack—for this kind of rapid, dry sauté—to develop the flavors without toughening the meat (especially when you're using temperamental veal). The dish also works well with boned chicken or fairly tender lamb cuts (sirloin end of leg) and beef (bottom sirloin). If the meat toughens on your first try, it will not be (you should excuse the expression) death in the pot. Just omit the olives, add some stock instead of the glacé, and braise it slowly until tender. (I'd advise having a standby steak at the ready if your first try is veal for a company meal). If your timing is accurate, every tender morsel will be glazed with an intensely meaty sweetness, nicely countered by the glazed olives (no gravy!).

YIELD: 4 servings

1½ lb. loin of veal, cut into 1-inch cubes
olive oil
2 Tbsp unsalted butter
1½ oz. minced onion
1½ oz. minced garlic
1 tsp dried marjoram
2½ oz. dry Marsala wine
16 drained giant green olives (not pitted)
½ cup veal demi-glacé

Dry meat well, but do not flour it. Use VERY HOT cast iron skillet. Sauté a small amount at a time in not-too-much olive oil. Fry until well colored or dry. Toss it—you will see flames.

Have ready a sautoir, sized to hold meat in one layer; position the sautoir so only half of it is over a burner with the heat turned off. As meat is browned, transfer it into the off-burner half of the sautoir pan. When all meat is browned, bring the sautoir to heat, put butter in the empty half of the pan, add minced garlic and onion, and sauté it in the half of the pan that's over the heat. Add marjoram and let all the flavors develop and cook into the veal, with the pan now moved to the center of the burner.

Add the Marsala and reduce it over high heat. If using olives, fold them in now. Add enough demi-glacé to glaze the meat well. Serve with Chef Aldo's Wild Rice (see page 116).

NOTE:

If you keep a veal-stock kitchen, here's a helpful hint from Chef Ron Barber: simmer stock with pot half off the burner. The albumin (the foamy scum) will accumulate on only half of the pot's surface, simplifying the constant skimming process.

SALADS

A SALAD OF CODDLED CHICKEN AND FINNOCCHIO

Now I'm going to tell you a way to cook chicken that may turn out to be one of the most frequently useful things you'll glean from these cookery notes—even if you're not counting anybody's calories.

YIELD: 4 entrée portions

1 2½- to 2¾-lb. broiler chicken
2 bulbs of fennel (finnocchio)
1 red bell pepper
1 bunch scallions, sliced thinly
lingonberry preserves
2 Tbsp thinly sliced cornichons (tiny dill gherkins)
¼-cup whole egg mayonnaise
juice of half a lime
lettuce cups, or 4 scooped-out poached apples

Clean the bird of all loose fat. Freeze the neck and innards for stock. Place the bird breast up in a pot that just fits, and which can be tightly covered. Add enough cold water to barely cover the bird, place the covered pot over a brisk flame, and set a timer for 15 minutes. When the timer rings, start peeking so you can catch the water the minute it starts to bubble. When the bubbles appear, quickly replace lid very tightly (and don't reopen it until the coddling is completed), lower the heat to simmer, and set the timer for 10 minutes, or 15 minutes, if chicken is 3 to 3½ lbs, at which time remove the covered pot to a 200° oven or warmer tray for one hour. Remove the bird, degrease

the cooking water and save it for stock (the flavor will be in the bird, not in the water). This method produces a most succulent, full-flavored poultry, to serve as is, or with condiments, or in a salad such as this one:

Cube all the skinned, boned, de-fatted meat, both light and dark, from the cooled, coddled chicken into a mixing bowl. I say two fennel bulbs because you want the upper, green stalks mixed with the white bulb, and they cut them so low it takes two bulbs to get a good mix of white and green for the heaping cupful the salad requires. Slice it very thinly. If you can't find a *red* bell pepper, just omit it—don't substitute. Cut pepper into small dice. Add thinly sliced scallions, 2 Tbsp drained fruits from a jar of lingonberries (or substitute whole cranberries from sauce, if you must), the sliced cornichons, and the mayonnaise, thinned out with fresh lime juice until thin enough to lightly coat, but still adhere to, the ingredients. Toss well.

Cram cooled cubed coddled chicken salad into the hollowed-out poached apples, or mound inside fluffy cups molded from outer leaves of lettuce.

NOTE:

Another way to use coddled chicken is to disjoint it, keep it refrigerated in a covered crock for a week, covered with white wine, garlic, and herbs, and serve cold, as Italian Drunken Chicken.

INSALATA DI PUNTETTE E PIGNOLI

A salad of puntette pasta and pine nuts, to serve with pâtés, cold cuts, cold roasts, and game

YIELD: 4 to 6 servings

¼ tsp salt
15 oz. water
4 level Tbsp frozen
    unsweetened orange
    juice concentrate
¼ tsp ground coriander
    seed
2 tsp crushed dried mint
    or applemint leaves
8 oz. puntette (or other
    rice-shaped pasta)
2 rounded Tbsp currants
1 fat clove garlic,
    pressed
6 scallions, including
    tops, thinly sliced
2 oz. whole pine nuts
½ Tbsp light olive oil
½ Tbsp pear vinegar
half a lime
1 thin slice prosciutto,
    cut into bits

In a heavy enameled pan with a tightly fitting lid, bring water to a boil with the salt, orange juice concentrate, coriander, and applemint leaves.

Have the pasta prewashed, by running cold water over it in a strainer until water runs clear. Add the washed pasta as soon as the liquid reaches boil, slowly, so as not to disturb the boil. Add the currants. Cover, and do not remove the cover until done. After 10 minutes, move still-covered pan to a cold back burner to sit undisturbed for an hour. Stir gently and refrigerate in a covered container.

Thirty minutes before serving, remove from the refrigerator, and fold in the garlic and scallions. Lightly sauté the pine nuts in olive oil and add to pasta. Add the mild vinegar, lime juice, and prosciutto bits to the pine nuts' sauté pan. Bring the pan back to heat, and pour dressing into pasta. Fold gently and serve in lettuce cups.

A SANDWICH AND A BREAD

FOCACCIA CHEESE SANDWICH

With all that lovely focaccia being turned out hot from the oven all day long around the corner from my house, why would I ever bother to make my own focaccia? Because this loaf form, with the cheese-softening carefully timed for insertion into the hand-burning, hot-from-the-oven loaf, is almost alchemy. It transforms bread and cheese into Goldensandwich.

YIELD: from 6 to 12 servings, according to its part in the meal

2 lbs. ripe teleme cheese, cut into ½-inch-thick slabs

¾ oz. (¾ of a cake) compressed cake yeast

½ cup warm water (80°–95°)

2 tsp honey

2 Tbsp olive oil

1 cup sifted unbleached flour

1 cup unsifted whole wheat flour

1 cup unsifted all-purpose white flour, plus extra for working the dough

olive oil

coarse salt

Bring the cheese to room temperature (about one hour). Bring the yeast cake to room temperature, then crumble three-fourths of it into a glass. Add the warm water and honey to the yeast. Let it stand 5 to 10 minutes until the mixture bubbles and rises in the glass. Add the olive oil.

Put unbleached flour and whole-wheat flour into the large bowl of an electric mixer. Add the yeast mixture and mix to blend. At medium speed, beat until the dough pulls away from the side of the bowl—about 5 minutes. If mixer has no dough hook, remove the bowl to the table and use a wooden spoon to stir in the white flour, ½ cup at a time, or until dough is stiff. Turn out onto a pastry board sprinkled with

¼-cup white flour, dip hands in flour, and knead dough 10 minutes, adding more white flour as needed, until the dough is rather soft but not sticky. Place the dough in an oiled bowl, cover it, and let it rise in draft-free warm place (about 85°) until doubled in size—about 1 hour at 85° (longer if the room is cooler). When the dough is punched with two fingers and the indentation remains, it's time to punch air bubbles out and shape the dough into three balls to fit 8-inch pie tins (or to lay out in 8-inch round loaves on oiled cookie sheet). At this point, you can wrap and freeze the raw loaves, to thaw and bake whenever you're ready.

Make indentations with fingertips one inch apart all over tops of loaves, to hold the oil and salt during baking. Brush tops with olive oil and sprinkle the coarse salt over them. Bake at 350° until golden brown—about 20 minutes. Halve each loaf horizontally while hot, lay a slab of cheese cut to fit on bottom halves, cover with top halves and quickly foil-wrap for 10 minutes. Immediately cut into wedges and serve.

NOTE:

If you bake loaves in clay pots, you'll more nearly approximate the bread texture that Sorocco's hearth ovens achieve. Don't make a loaf smaller than 8 inches, or you'll have too much crust in proportion to the soft insides, more like a foccacetta than focaccia.

VEGETABLES

THE NORTH BEACH STIR-FRY

And, because the North Beach Italians live hand-in-pocket with their Chinese neighbors, we have the North Beach Stir-Fry. Assuming that you have the stir-fry technique in your repertory, I'll merely suggest some ways to get out your wok and think Italian.

Heat the wok. Dribble chosen cooking oil into the wok from the top edges down. Stir-fry mashed chopped garlic and discard garlic. Stir-fry whole sprigs of fresh herbs (such as oregano, rosemary, marjoram, or thyme) and discard the sprigs. Stir-fry prepared vegetables, putting the longest-cooking ones into the wok first. Add seasoned liquid mixture (the wine of your choice, with the appropriate stock; potato, corn or arrowroot starch; perhaps a spice; and—when cooking either tomatoes, peas, or meats—a pinch of sugar). Bring the liquid to a boil, cover the wok, lower the heat, and simmer a couple minutes.

Some notions for combining, to get you started:

Spinach, pine nuts, raisins, Marsala wine (corn oil and garlic).

Mushrooms (fresh and soaked dry ones, the more kinds the merrier), with shallots, leeks, and 2-inch scallion pieces (olive oil, garlic, and marjoram; veal stock with vermouth and brandy).

Olive oil, garlic, long strips of fennel, red bell peppers, red onions, long strips of fresh tomato, and anchovy mashed into a little pesto base and mixed with chicken stock, Campari and brandy, a sprinkle of capers.

Olive oil, oregano, garlic, zucchini, Italian green beans, red onion, cherry tomatoes, a touch of tomato paste mixed in beef stock and port.

SOME GARNISHES: scallion slices, coarsely chopped Italian flat-leafed parsley, sweet basil, capers, walnuts dipped in buckwheat flour and eggwhite and deep fried, sautéed pine nuts.

SPAGHETTI SQUASH

A relatively new vegetable in our markets, these elongated yellow-beige squash weigh about two to four pounds each, and have more to do with texture than taste. The cooked spaghetti-like strands have a consistency somewhere between vegetables and cellophane noodles, and are interesting to experiment with.

TO BAKE: Pierce a 3½- to 4-lb. squash in several places and bake in a shallow pan in a 350° oven for 1½ hours or until the shell gives to a gentle pressure. Cut in half lenthwise, discard the seeds, and loosen the strands. The squash is now ready to be seasoned and served— combined with other foods, in casseroles, soups, or with sauce or compound butter.

SUGGESTED SEASONINGS: Garlic butter, basil butter, Piedmont butter (see page 129), butter, grated cheese, salt and pepper, a cheese sauce, pesto sauce, tomato or meat sauce.

DESSERTS

CHEF EDGAR ROJAS' FRIED CREAM

The traditional North Beach dessert, Edgar's way

YIELD: 6 servings

24 oz. (3 cups) milk
4 oz. (¼ cup) sugar,
less 1 tsp
8 oz. (1 level cup)
semolina
2 egg yolks, well beaten
1 oz. (2 Tbsp) unsalted
butter, softened
1 Tbsp Cointreau
2 large sugar cubes
1 orange
whites of 2 eggs, plus
one whole egg,
beaten well
fine dry bread crumbs
6 shots warmed cognac
oil to deep-fry

Bring milk to its boiling point in a heavy, 2-quart saucepan. Immediately lower it to a simmer. Gradually add mixture of sugar with semolina, stirring into the simmering milk. Stir for about 20 minutes, until the mixture thickens to dense. Remove from heat.

Rub the sugar cubes on all sides over the dry skin of an orange, until cubes absorb the oil of the orange skin. Over low heat, melt the impregnated cubes in the Cointreau, without letting the Cointreau boil. Use a flame-tamer or asbestos pad if needed.

Beat into the dense mixture the egg yolks, softened butter, and the Cointreau preparation. Pour into an oblong pan which is at least 2 inches deep, but not so long that the mixture won't be at least 1½ inches high. Have the pan cold, and dip it in cold water to moisten, before you pour the custard into it. Refrigerate overnight. The custard will keep in the refrigerator, covered with waxpaper and a damp cloth, for several days.

TO SERVE: Cut the custard into 1½-inch squares. Dip each square into the beaten egg to coat, then into crumbs (crumbed melba toast does well). When all the squares are coated, quickly deep-fry in batches until all are golden brown. Drain on paper towels. Put two squares in each shallow serving dish, pour a shot of cognac over each serving, and carefully ignite. Serve flaming.

BAKED STUFFED PEARS

YIELD: 6 servings

6 large, sound pears, peeled and cored (cut ¾-inch cavities)
1 oz. bittersweet chocolate, chopped
6 fresh small almond (not coconut) macaroons
2 oz. heavy cream
panettone, sliced ½-inch thick
a scant cup sauterne
2 Tbsp butter

Preheat the oven to 325°. Select six individual baking cups, sized to hold each pear upright. Cut panettone slices to fit the bottoms of the cups, butter the bread slices on one side and put them, buttered side down, into the cups.

Set a pear in each cup, and stuff each pear with a coarsely crumbled fresh almond macaroon. Push it in tightly, and top with some chopped chocolate, until pear is filled to the top; spoon a little cream over all of this.

Pour the sauterne around the pears and bake uncovered for 50 minutes. Then, spoon a little more heavy cream over each pear and bake for another 10 minutes.

Serve hot in the baking dishes and pass a pitcher of cold heavy cream.

About the Authors

Brian St. Pierre grew up around his family's restaurant business in
Boston. A professional food and wine writer, he is currently Public
Relations Director of the San Francisco Wine Institute and a Member
of the Society of Wine Educators. His extensive professional travels
have convinced him that North Beach is the most interesting and
accessible "Little Italy" in the United States, full of unexpected
rewards for native and visitor alike.

One of Mary Etta Moose's Sicilian great-grandfathers was chef to the
Cardinal of Naples. A renowned chef in her own right, she has
noodled around North Beach for twenty years. Working with the
venerable *Capi-di-Cuccina* of North Beach in her capacity as Manager of
Cuisine at Washington Square Bar & Grill, she has acquired an extensive knowledge of the complexities of food preparation and combination that mark this pocket of original Italian-American cuisine.

A NOTE ON THE TYPE

The type in this book was set in Bembo. The famous Venetian printer Aldus Manutius commissioned Francesco Griffo of Bologna to cut the face for an edition of *De Aetna* by the humanist scholar Pietro Bembo in 1495. The modern adaptation of this fine letter was produced in the 1920s for the English Monotype Corporation. This face is an accurate photocomposed version.